BECOMING A PUBLIC INTEREST LAWYER

Nicole Hallett
Clinical Professor of Law
The University of Chicago Law School

WEST ACADEMIC PUBLISHING

444 Cedar Street, Suite 700
St. Paul, MN 55101
1-877-888-1330

Printed in the United States of America

ISBN: 978-1-63659-770-6

To my husband, without whom my career as a public interest lawyer and this book would have been impossible.

To my children, for whom I wake up each day striving to make the world a better place.

ACKNOWLEDGMENTS

I would like to thank my current and former students who read and commented on drafts of this book, including Erin Barry, Jordan Jenkins, Fernando Stepansky, Alice Thompson, Sage Garcia, Allison O'Connor, Brenda Garcia, and Meghfira Mohammed.

I would also like to thank the professors who mentored me when I was a law student and set me on my path to becoming a public interest lawyer, including Michael Wishnie, Harold Koh, and Stephen Wizner.

About the Author

Nicole Hallett is a Clinical Professor of Law at the University of Chicago Law School. After graduating from Yale Law School, she clerked on the U.S. Court of Appeals for the Second Circuit and the U.S. District Court for the District of Connecticut. She began her public interest career as a Skadden Fellow and then a staff attorney at the Urban Justice Center in New York City. She has taught at Yale Law School, where she was a Robert M. Cover Fellow, as well as at NYU School of Law and the University at Buffalo School of Law. Nicole blogs about public interest lawyering at Blog for the Public Good, www.blogforthepublicgood.com. She lives in Chicago with her husband and two children.

TABLE OF CONTENTS

BECOMING A PUBLIC INTEREST LAWYER

CHAPTER 1

INTRODUCTION

This book is for aspiring lawyers, current law students and practicing attorneys who want to pursue careers in public interest law. It starts from the premise that *anyone* can succeed in having a fulfilling and meaningful public interest legal career. It supplements and corrects what public interest students are taught before and during law school. Legal education has evolved dramatically in recent decades and more attention is paid to public interest law than ever before. Still, students often must search out the information they need to succeed on the public interest job market. The knowledge gets conveyed in individual conversations behind closed doors to those who know to seek it out or it is learned through trial and error. There is no reason that it must be this way. Every law student should have the tools they need to get the job they want.

The book takes a journey with an aspiring public interest lawyer, from deciding whether to go to law school to the job search process and everything in-between. Every chapter provides concrete advice that you can put to use immediately. Anyone who wants to become a public interest lawyer—from the college student just thinking about law school to the mid-career lawyer who wants to make a career change—can benefit from this book. However, it will be most useful for people just beginning their law school careers.

The book also will help you determine which kind of public interest law is the right fit for you by exploring the different kinds of public interest jobs that exist. Although public interest jobs all have something in common—they all strive to advance the public good in some way—the day-to-day work varies considerably. No public interest job is the same as any other. Different jobs require different competencies and present different challenges. Many students come to law school with a clear sense for what they want to do—until they actually spend some time in that job. Other students may feel unmoored, wanting to use their law degree for good but without a clear sense for how. This book is a resource for anyone who needs some guidance on which public interest job to pursue.

Finally, the book lays out common mistakes that law students make that can derail their plans and provides strategies that they can use to prevent these missteps from happening. A large proportion of incoming law students plan to pursue public interest careers, but by graduation only a small fraction will take public interest jobs. A recent study by the American Bar Association (ABA) found that 67% of law school applicants are interested in law school because they are committed to social change or want to help other people. At graduation, however, less than 8% take public interest jobs.[1] For the most part, law students abandon their public interest goals for reasons that have little to do with their internal desires and motivations. Instead, a combination of incentives and institutional inertia leads law students on career paths very different than the ones they thought they would pursue.

I have been a practicing public interest lawyer for fifteen years. When I applied to law school, I knew very little about the legal profession and had no idea about what kinds of legal careers existed. I would not have been able to tell you what the average salary for a lawyer was and I had given very little thought to how I was going to pay off my law schools loans. The one thing I knew was that I wanted to help people and I thought that law school would allow me to do that. When I arrived on campus, I found many of my classmates had similar aspirations.

Three years later, many of these same classmates had accepted jobs at corporate law firms. Quite a few are still there. This collective decision to abandon public interest law was nothing short of bewildering to me at the time. In retrospect, though, it is unsurprising. Without guidance and support, many students find it impossible to remain committed to public interest law.

I took a different path. I muddled through law school with a lot of mentorship and some luck, and I resisted the siren call of corporate law. After clerking for two years, I became a public interest lawyer at a non-profit organization in New York City. I

[1] American Bar Association, Profile of the Legal Profession 58 (2021).

am now a clinical professor at the University of Chicago Law School, where I spend a lot of my time advising and mentoring law students and young lawyers. They have some of the same questions I did, as well as some questions that I was too naïve to ask. This book will attempt to provide answers to these questions.

WHAT IS PUBLIC INTEREST LAW

Before discussing public interest lawyering, we first need to define what it is. Public interest law is a common term that does not have a settled definition. Practically speaking, people tend to think of it in terms of the different categories of public interest employers, such as non-profit organizations; federal, state, or local governments; public-private law firms; social entrepreneurship; and academia. These are useful categories because each requires different preparation and are quite distinct in how lawyers in these jobs spend their days. You will see these categories referenced throughout the book.

On a more conceptual level, public interest law is both broader and narrower than these categories suggest. One common definition is any legal work that has as one of its stated goals the advancement of the public good. Some definitions also include a requirement that the work not be undertaken for a remunerative purpose, which distinguishes public interest law from most other legal work that is done for financial gain.

This definition is not without its problems. Most obviously, what is in the public interest is hotly contested. There are many issues where lawyers on both sides believe quite fervently that they are acting in the public interest despite having diametrically opposed goals. Lawyers on both sides of an issue can be motivated by principles of equality and justice. They simply disagree about how to interpret what those principles mean.

The approach this book takes is to define what is in the public interest by looking at the intent of those doing the work rather than by making independent normative judgments about its value. This definition allows readers to make their own judgments and leaves broader discussions about what exactly is in the public interest for another day.

However, this book rejects the notion that public interest lawyers cannot take financial considerations into account when deciding what legal work to take on. Public interest law should not require lawyers to take a vow of poverty. There are many lawyers who make good money while also contributing to the public good, and such work should be encouraged, not dismissed. If one of the primary goals of the work is to contribute to the public good, this book will consider it public interest law. Some private sector work meets this definition and is included in the book for this reason.

As you read, you should think about how *you* define public interest law and which of the many possible career paths will allow you to feel like you are contributing to the public good. The most important thing you can do is ask yourself this question.

WHY STUDENTS GIVE UP ON THEIR PUBLIC INTEREST DREAMS

For students who come to law school with the plan to go into public interest law, law school can be disorienting and discouraging. Lots of public interest dreams die or are deferred. Of course, some students simply change their minds about what they want to do and are very happy with their choices. But many students regret being diverted from the reason they came to law school. There are three key reasons that this happens: law school culture, the personality traits of many law students, and financial necessity. If you are aware of these forces before you start law school, you have a better chance of resisting them.

The Moving Walkway

Law school is like a moving walkway that students step on as soon as they arrive that leads them to take jobs in corporate law after law school. This happens for several reasons—everyone else is stepping on, the school is encouraging it, and, simply put, it is easier than forging your own path.

The peculiar thing about public interest jobs is that while they pay less than private sector jobs, they are harder to get. Students are wined and dined at law firm receptions. They then apply for law firm jobs through on-campus interviewing programs in which a student can interview with many firms without doing much more than submitting a resume. Firms make it easy for students to stay on the moving walkway once they have stepped on. They lure students to accept summer positions by paying them more than most students have made in their entire lives. By the end of their second summer, most summer associates have an offer in hand for after graduation. At that point, it is hard to turn down.

Students who are interested in public interest jobs must work much harder. A few organizations may participate in on-campus interviewing, but most do not. They may only hire one or two interns each summer, as opposed to law firms that often hire dozens of summer associates. Students must craft individualized cover letters and applications for each internship. Non-profit organizations expect applicants not only to have excellent grades, but also to express enthusiasm for and, ideally, have experience in the specific sub-area of law in which the organization works. Moreover, summer public interest internships—which are usually unpaid—do not tend to lead to permanent job offers. Instead, students must go through another round of applications for public interest fellowships and entry-level jobs. These fellowships and jobs are even rarer than the internships students applied for a year earlier. In these circumstances, it is not surprising that many law students give up and take a law firm job.

Law schools could try to be a counterbalance to these incentives, and they do to an extent. Some law schools, for example, provide post-graduation fellowships for students so that they can work at non-profit organizations for one or two years. These fellowships are critical to jump-starting public interest careers. But most law schools are more than happy to see most of their graduates go work in the private sector. To understand why, you have to understand the different interests of law schools and their students.

Let's start with your interests as a law student. When you are thinking about what job you want to take after graduation, you may have many considerations in mind. You want a job that is fulfilling and challenging, but that allows you to have a good work-life balance. You may be thinking about having a family and may decide on a career path based partly on which job makes that feasible. You also want to live a good life, which probably requires a decent salary. At the very least, you need to be able to afford your loan payments and basic living expenses. You might also be looking for a job that gives you a sense of purpose and allows you to contribute something important in the world. There may be no job that allows you to balance all of these considerations perfectly, but they all may influence which job you end up taking.

Now let's turn to the interests of law schools. They may say that they have the same goals as their students and that they are trying to make sure every student finds the job of their dreams after graduation. Of course they say that! Students are customers and they are trying to convince students to enroll at their school rather than somewhere else.

But law schools' institutional interests differ in several important respects. First and foremost, they want to make sure that as many of their graduates as possible are employed in legal jobs ten months after graduation, because that is one of the statistics that U.S. News and World Report uses to determine law school rankings. It requires fewer career development resources to get students jobs in the private sector than it does to help them get public interest jobs. Moreover, they have an incentive to encourage students to take the first job offer they get because then they can focus their resources on the remaining students without jobs. As an added incentive, the higher the average salary is of their graduating class, the more alumni resources are likely to flow back to the law school in perpetuity. Higher salaries also allow schools to charge more in tuition. The average total cost of a law school degree is now more than $200,000,[2] which can only be justified if the salaries that graduates can expect are similarly high.

Why is it, then, that law schools spend resources developing their public interest programs? Because their incentives are different when they are recruiting students than when they are placing them in jobs. Remember, many prospective law students *want* to pursue public interest careers and those students are

[2] Education Data Initiative, Average Cost of Law School, https://educationdata.org/average-cost-of-law-school (last accessed May 27, 2022).

choosing law schools in part based on their public interest programs.

In other words, if law schools made decisions based on their own interests (rather than the interests of their students) you would see public-facing public interest programs as well as institutional pressure for students to choose private sector employment once they matriculate. Ideally, they would also have a few students who successfully get public interest jobs because the example of those students is important for recruitment purposes.

Unsurprisingly, that is precisely what we see. As Professor Bill Quigley wrote in his *Letter to a Law Student Interested in Social Justice*, though law schools pay lip service to public interest, "[t]he actual message from law school and on throughout the entire legal career is that justice work, if done at all, is done in the margins or after the real legal work is done."[3] A student who comes to law school wanting to do public interest law faces strong headwinds.

The law school curriculum further entrenches this ethos. The case method, which has dominated legal pedagogy for over a hundred years, teaches students how to explain legal rules, not critique them. Students are indoctrinated into legal systems, not taught how to change them. In fact, research has shown that increased reliance on the case method as a mode of teaching decreases law students' feelings of moral certitude and political engagement.[4] Private law courses form the backbone of the first-year curriculum. Topics related to justice and equality are relegated to electives or not taught at all. This way of teaching law is changing, but slowly. A student who comes to law school wanting to be a public interest lawyer will likely find very little in their first year of law school that inspires them. It gets easier after that first year, but by then many law students are already off track. The first thing many law students lose that first year is the reason why they came.[5]

---

[3] William P. Quigley, *Letter to a Law Student Interested in Social Justice*, 1 DEPAUL J. FOR SOC. JUST. 7, 11 (2007).

[4] ALAN K. CHEN & SCOTT L. CUMMINGS, PUBLIC INTEREST LAWYERING 404 (2013).

[5] Quigley, *supra* note 3, at 8.

This does not mean that there are not individual professors and staff who are committed to helping students on the path to rewarding public interest legal careers. They exist at every law school. But it is difficult for those individuals to completely counteract the institutional culture that law students regularly encounter. Students must insulate themselves from this culture, while actively seeking out the support they need to succeed. This would be difficult to do in normal circumstances. For students already stressed by law school itself, it can end up feeling impossible.

It is no wonder that many of the best and brightest students who go to law school will come out with an offer from a corporate law firm even if that was not their initial goal. Each individual student may have compelling reasons to abandon their public interest goals. But when so many people make the same decision, there must be institutional factors at play. Almost every incentive is pushing in one direction. In this environment, it is unsurprising that public interest students lose their way.

The Pursuit of Gold Stars

The second reason law students give up on public interest law has to do with the fact that law school attracts the kind of person who is particularly vulnerable to the pressures outlined above. To get in to law school, you must have a strong undergraduate record, which means most aspiring lawyers are hardworking, ambitious, and high achieving. People who go to law school also tend to be risk averse and inclined to follow the rules. Law is quite literally a system of rules that govern society and lawyers become custodians of this system. Rebels and revolutionaries are unlikely to find the legal profession a compelling career path. This does not describe every lawyer, but anyone who has gone to law school knows that people that match this description outnumber those who do not.

What ambitious, risk-averse people want more than anything else is gold stars, those markers of achievement that identify them as a success. Throughout high school and college, these gold stars take the form of awards, scholarships, and letters of admission. To get these gold stars, young people need good grades and high test scores, but that is usually not sufficient. They also need to show dedication to extra-curricular activities such as sports, the arts, and volunteer work. The last of these is designed to demonstrate a person's commitment to public service, which is often one of the criteria for earning these gold stars. Requirements of this type exist throughout high school and college, up and through applying for law school. For students who are interested in public service, their passions are in line with their ambitions. Their commitment is not only intrinsically worthwhile, but it also allows them to successfully pursue extrinsic markers of success.

In law school, however, the gold stars start to change. There are no more schools to apply for, no more scholarships to win. Suddenly everyone is boasting about offers from corporate law firms. People begin to compete over things like salaries and corporate perks, and then later, over wine cellars, beach houses, and penthouse apartments. These things are not only valued for their own sake, but also for the status they confer. Status, it turns out, is the ultimate gold star.

An aspiring public interest lawyer must resist the urge to compete for these gold stars. But they are often the kind of person for whom gold stars are irresistible. In the end, their motivation and drive to succeed often wins out over their noble aspirations for going to law school, aspirations that until then have been encouraged and nurtured by the gold star system.

Student Loans

The final reason students abandon public interest law is debt. The average law school graduate has $160,000 in loans at graduation.[6] This number has almost doubled in the past twenty years.[7] Law schools are not the only ones with a student debt problem, which has plagued all corners of higher education and has led to national calls for reform and debt relief.[8] A policy fix is the only way to truly solve this problem, but individuals must still make decisions about their careers in the meantime. And

---

[6] Education Data Initiative, https://educationdata.org/average-law-school-debt (last accessed May 17, 2022).

[7] *Id.*

[8] Ron Lieber, *Student Loan Borrowers Don't Deserve 'Forgiveness.' They Deserve an Apology.* N.Y. TIMES, May 13, 2022, https://www.nytimes.com/2022/05/13/your-money/student-loan-forgiveness.html.

there is no doubt that debt plays a major role in which career paths law students choose. The most common reason given for why law students change their minds about going into public interest law is that they are worried about not being able to pay their loans.[9]

It is possible to become a public interest lawyer even if you have student loans, but that is not the lesson that law students learn from their schools and their peers. Soon after matriculation, the drum beat of anxiety over student loans begins. Older students will explain that they are going to work for a law firm for a few years "to pay off their loans." Rumors will circulate that only independently wealthy students can afford to go into public interest law. Each disbursement causes dread and worry about being unable to pay it all back. Career development offices do not discourage this catastrophic thinking, happily encouraging students to defer what they really want to do for a few years until their loans are paid off. You may hear so often that you must pay off your loans before taking a public interest job that you begin to believe it.

A DIFFERENT PERSPECTIVE

All these factors make law school a challenging experience for aspiring public interest lawyers. But with the right tools and information, you can overcome these challenges. By understanding the pressures you are likely to face in law school, you are more likely to be able to resist them. By understanding yourself and the reasons why you may be diverted from your goals, you will be able to choose your career path deliberately and purposefully. By coming up with a plan for how you are going to pay off your law school loans, you will be able to reduce the anxiety that causes many students to take high-paying corporate jobs they do not want. With these obstacles out of the way, you will be able to choose your career path, not have one foisted on you by circumstances that feel out of your control.

It should be clear by now that I approach this topic from a particular perspective. If you are looking for a book that validates your choices, whatever they may be, you are probably in the wrong place. You will likely hear competing advice from

---

[9] CHEN & CUMMINGS, *supra* note 4 at 409.

other people, and it is always important to get multiple points of view. This book represents my point of view as well as that of a significant number of my peers who are practicing public interest lawyers.

Full disclosure: I think being a public interest lawyer is one of the best jobs in the world. You get to wake up every day knowing that your work matters. You are changing lives and if you are lucky, you are making the world a better place. The struggle to get a public interest job is real, but it is worth it. I hope this book helps you make it happen.

CHAPTER 2

PUBLIC INTEREST JOBS

When most people envision public interest lawyers, they usually think of lawyers working at legal aid organizations. However, being a legal aid attorney is only one of many different options for people who want to go into public interest law. All public interest jobs are united in their motivation (to advance the public interest) but differ considerably in what the day-to-day work looks like and in what they are trying to accomplish. If you want to be a public interest lawyer, you will need to figure out what job is right for you. Here are a few of the different kinds of public interest jobs you should consider.

NON-PROFIT ORGANIZATIONS

Not all non-profit organizations are the same. They can have distinct missions and devote themselves to a wide variety of work. Although the diversity of non-profit organizations is endless, there are certain categories of organization that you will encounter repeatedly. Even if you have decided that you want to work at a non-profit organization, you will still need to decide which kind of organization you want to work at. Each type of organization plays an important role in the public interest ecosystem.[1]

Legal Aid

Legal aid organizations are non-profits that provide pro bono legal services to individuals with low incomes who cannot afford to pay for a lawyer. Common practice areas include housing, custody and divorce, domestic violence, disability and welfare benefits, consumer debt, bankruptcy, employment, juvenile delinquency, expungement, and clemency. The work may be litigation (legal work that involves courts) or transactional (legal work that involves dealings between people

---

[1] For a history of the different models of public interest lawyering and the disputes that have arisen between adherents of the different models, see Rebecca Sharpless, *More Than One Lane Wide: Against Hierarchies of Helping in Progressive Legal Advocacy*, 19 CLINICAL L. REV. 347 (2012).

or entities). Legal aid organizations usually focus on areas of law in which low-income individuals are disproportionately or solely impacted, and not on other areas of law affecting people of all income levels, such as personal injury or business incorporation. Because public defender offices typically represent indigent people in criminal proceedings, legal aid organizations usually focus primarily on civil matters, though they may do work at the intersection of criminal and civil legal systems such as post-conviction relief or legal issues related to reentry after incarceration. Lawyers at these organizations sometimes specialize in one area of law, but in smaller organizations they might need to be generalists.

These organizations vary in where their funding comes from, which in turn controls what work they can do. Some organizations are funded by the Legal Services Corporation (LSC), a federally-funded non-profit created in the 1974 with the mission of providing civil legal services to low-income persons. LSC receives money from the federal government and then distributes it to 132 organizations across the country.[2] LSC-funded organizations are limited to helping individuals making less than 125% of the federal poverty line.[3]

During the 1970s and 80s, LSC-funded organizations came under scrutiny for engaging in impact litigation and other law reform projects.[4] In response, Congress enacted a series of restrictions on the kind of work that LSC-funded organizations can undertake. Today, organizations that accept LSC funds cannot participate in any class action lawsuit, conduct advocacy training on public policy issues, or attempt to influence regulatory, legislative, or adjudicative action at the federal, state, or local level. They are also limited in which issues they can work on and whom they can represent. LSC-funded organizations cannot represent certain categories of non-citizens, engage in litigation related to abortion, engage in litigation related to school desegregation, engage in litigation

---

[2] Legal Services Corporation, About LSC, https://www.lsc.gov/about-lsc (last accessed May 17, 2022).

[3] Legal Services Corporation, What is Legal Aid, https://www.lsc.gov/about-lsc/what-legal-aid (last accessed May 17, 2022).

[4] Alan Houseman & Linda E. Perle, Securing Equal Justice for All: A Brief History of Civil Legal Assistance in the United States 30 (2018).

related to draft registration or desertion from the military, represent clients in eviction proceedings if the eviction was based on drug-related activities; represent federal, state, or local prisoners, participate in efforts to reform a federal or state welfare system, or engage in activities related to assisted suicide, euthanasia, or mercy killing.[5]

Some legal aid organizations have decided not to accept LSC funds so that they do not have to comply with these restrictions. Others have separately incorporated non-LSC departments that can engage in otherwise prohibited activities. It is difficult to know which organizations are LSC funded and which are not from the outside. In some places, organizations with "legal services" in their names are LSC funded and others with "legal aid" in their name are not, but that is not always true. An organization's website may or may not specify how it is funded. If it is important to you not to be restricted in the kind of legal assistance you can provide to clients, you will want to know whether an organization you are considering is LSC funded or not. The best way to figure out whether an organization is LSC funded is to ask directly.

Non-LSC-funded organizations usually rely on a combination of state and local funding, foundations, law firms, and private donors to fund their organizations. In all fifty states, the District of Columbia, and Puerto Rico, Interest on Lawyer Trust Accounts (IOLTA) provides substantial funding for civil legal services. IOLTA funds are collected from lawyer trust accounts and then distributed to fund local non-profit organizations.[6]

Civil legal services are massively underfunded in the United States. Even LSC-funded organizations only get a small portion of their funding from LSC and must engage in outside fundraising. An attorney at a legal aid organization may need to spend time engaged in fundraising activities as well as grant reporting. In smaller organizations, this can eat up a substantial

---

5 Congressional Research Service, Legal Services Corporation: Restrictions on Activities 2 (2009), https://www.everycrsreport.com/files/20091222_R40679_981bee9f40dca63e628d6d36d7b7b6e5d0a6f951.pdf.

6 American Bar Association, Interest on Lawyer Trust Accounts, https://www.americanbar.org/groups/interest_lawyers_trust_accounts/overview (last accessed May 24, 2022).

portion of an attorney's time. Before accepting a job at a legal aid organization, you will want to inquire into how much fundraising and grant reporting the position requires. These non-legal tasks will reduce the number of clients you can serve.

Because many grants and other funding sources require legal aid organizations to assist a certain number of individuals in order to receive funding, they must prioritize assisting as many people as possible. That may mean that attorneys feel obligated to turn down more complicated cases that would require more resources. Like public defenders, legal aid attorneys often feel overburdened and under resourced. Some legal aid attorneys end up feeling like they are trying to bail out a sinking ship with a teaspoon. Burnout is a common problem.

However, if you are a person who enjoys interacting with people and who wants to see the impact of their work on a daily basis, there is no better place to work than a legal aid organization. For example, it may take decades to reform public housing, but the satisfaction of preventing an individual family from being evicted is immediate. A legal aid organization may also be a good fit for a lawyer who would like to specialize in more than one area of law. Clients often have multiple legal problems and legal aid lawyers are often tasked with providing wholistic legal services.

Legal aid attorneys usually spend a good portion of their time doing intakes and meetings with clients. Because the legal work they do is less likely to involve novel legal issues, they will spend disproportionately less time on legal research and brief writing. They are required to keep many balls in the air and are likely to work on multiple matters in a single day. If you are someone who enjoys solitary work or deep thinking and reflection, a legal aid organization may not be the right place for you. But if you get excited about solving concrete problems for real people, it might be. Legal aid organizations can be a terrific place to begin your career because you will get a lot of responsibility and gain lawyering skills immediately. It is less common for lawyers to transition into a legal aid job after a stint in another kind of job, though it does happen.

During the hiring process, legal aid organizations are often focused on identifying which candidates will be able to handle the unique stresses of legal aid jobs, including the high case load, client demands, and risk of burnout.

Impact Litigation

Organizations that do impact litigation differ in many ways from legal aid organizations. First, there are fewer of these organizations. You may be familiar with some of the biggest ones such as the ACLU, the NAACP, and Lambda Legal, but there are smaller organizations in every state. Some are part of larger organizations that do non-legal work as well (such as Planned Parenthood or the Sierra Club). Some exist as separate entities that engage solely in legal and/or advocacy work. Most are organized around a single issue or set of issues. Helping individual clients, though still a goal, is secondary to the primary goal of reforming the law through litigation.

Some good examples of impact litigation are the gender discrimination cases that Ruth Bader Ginsburg litigated during her time at the ACLU Women's Rights Project. She chose her clients carefully, famously bringing legal challenges on behalf of men victimized by gender discrimination under federal benefits statute.[7] It is very unlikely that Ginsburg thought that discrimination against men was the most pressing gender justice issue of the time. Still, she pursued this strategy because she believed that it maximized the odds that her long-term project of enshrining equal protection for women in the Constitution would be successful. It worked. A legal aid lawyer would not have been able to make these sorts of strategic choices. Instead, they would have been forced to represent whatever client walked in the door or might not have been able to press the issue at all given the complicated and novel legal issues involved.

The funding structure of impact organizations differs from legal aid as well. They are not LSC-funded and typically do not accept funding that requires them to represent a certain number of people. For this reason, they are more likely to rely on membership dues and individual donations than legal aid organizations. These organizations know that the more press

7 Ria Tabacca Mar, *Ruth Bader Ginsburg's Fight for Gender Equity Was For All of Us*, SCOTUS BLOG, Sept. 21, 2020, available at https://www.scotusblog.com/2020/09/ruth-bader-ginsburgs-fight-for-gender-equity-was-for-all-of-us.

and media their cases get, the more donations will roll in. Thus, there is a premium placed on publicity and on bringing high-profile cases.

Impact organizations are likely to take on fewer cases with more complex legal issues. A lawyer may only be working on a few cases at one time but be devoting substantial resources to each of them. Case selection is one of the most important responsibilities of an impact litigator. If a case gets bogged down in factual disputes, then the impact litigator has picked the wrong case. It is the legal issue above all else that motivates impact organizations.

Impact litigators do have clients, of course, but clients are often seen as distractions, not the focus of the case. Sometimes impact organizations co-counsel with legal aid lawyers so that they can outsource most, if not all, of the client contact. This aspect of impact litigation has garnered substantial criticism from lawyers who believe in client-centered practice. Impact litigators are also sometimes criticized as being disconnected from the communities they purport to speak for.[8] Still, for those who believe in law reform through litigation, there is nothing more rewarding than being an impact litigator.

The day-to-day work of an impact litigator is often focused on mapping out litigation strategy, researching and writing briefs, and arguing cases. Later in their career, an impact litigator may spend more time doing public advocacy around their legal issue. If you are someone who likes to feel a personal connection to clients, then impact litigation may not be for you. If you are someone who dislikes brief-writing and who hated moot court in law school, you should probably look elsewhere. If you are a creative thinker, a good writer, and an effective oral advocate, then impact litigation may be a good fit, especially if there is an issue or issues that you feel especially passionate about.

Lawyers sometimes transition to impact litigation after several years at a legal aid organization, though it is possible to get a job at one of these organizations directly out of law school.

---

[8] *See, e.g.*, Martha Gómez, *The Culture of Non-Profit Impact Litigation*, 23 CLINICAL L. REV. 635 (2017).

The focus in hiring at these organizations is often less about competence and more about identifying brilliant, innovative legal minds. Some organizations can be insular, only hiring lawyers who previously worked for them as interns or fellows. A law student who wants to go into impact litigation will likely need to prove themselves before applying, either by excelling in a different context or by making personal connections within the organization.

Law and Organizing

Also called movement lawyering or community lawyering, law and organizing is a relatively new kind of public interest law. Organizations that engage in law and organizing provide legal services in support of and in collaboration with community groups and other grassroots organizations dedicated to social change.[9]

Law and organizing arose in the 1980s and 1990s because of disillusionment with more traditional forms of lawyering, which were focused almost exclusively on using the legal system to advance social justice goals. Lawyers who practice law and organizing understand the importance of courts, but do not believe that courts drive social change. Instead, they believe that courts lag behind changes that occur in the culture and in society at large. The role of the lawyer is also different. Movement lawyers see themselves playing supporting, not starring, roles in social movements, as Jennifer Gordon explains in her article, "The Lawyer is Not the Protagonist."[10] This role may be hard to swallow for lawyers who have been steeped in traditional legal culture, which idolizes famous advocates and judges.

The potential conflict between traditional lawyering and a movement-based approach is illustrated in the fight to legalize gay marriage.[11] The LGBTQ+ advocacy community had made a strategic decision to focus on state-level legislation rather than

9 Scott L. Cummings & Ingrid V. Eagley, *A Critical Reflection On Law And Organizing*, 48 UCLA L. REV. 443, 493–96 (2001)

10 Jennifer Gordon, *Concluding Essay: The Lawyer Is Not the Protagonist: Community Campaigns, Law, and Social Change*, 95 CAL. L. REV. 2133 (2007).

11 Dale Carpenter, *On the Legal Front Lines of Same-Sex Marriage*, N.Y. TIMES, June 29, 2014, https://www.nytimes.com/2014/06/30/books/redeeming-the-dream-by-theodore-b-olson-and-david-boies.html.

federal court challenges because of the belief that the Supreme Court was unlikely to get ahead of public opinion on the issue. For years, this strategy worked as gay marriage was legalized on a state-by-state basis. Enter David Boies and Ted Olsen, Supreme Court litigators who had previously argued both sides of *Bush v. Gore* in 2000. When in 2009 Boies and Olsen filed a constitutional challenge to Prop 8, the referendum that had overturned the California law allowing same sex marriage, only three other states had legalized gay marriage: Massachusetts, Connecticut, and Iowa. The LGBTQ+ advocacy community opposed the lawsuit and believed that bringing the issue before the Supreme Court too early would result in an adverse decision that could harm the movement for a generation or more. Boies and Olsen refused to listen.

By the time the case got to the Supreme Court in 2013, however, nine states had legalized gay marriage. By the time the Supreme Court decided *Obergefell v. Hodges* legalizing gay marriage nationwide two years later, 37 states had legalized gay marriage. This anecdote is a little like a Rorschach test. What you see depends on which theory of change you believe in. Did the Supreme Court legalize gay marriage because cultural attitudes had shifted, or did cultural attitudes shift because courts had begun to rule in favor of same sex marriage? The LGBTQ+ community has one answer to that question, Boies and Olsen another. If you believe in law and organizing, however, the answer is clear. Courts followed public opinion. They did not shape it.

Law and organizing can still take the form of litigation, although it will likely be connected to a larger campaign or organizing movement. It can also take the form of legal clinics and community education designed to empower communities with information. It may take the form of providing legal advice to the organization itself in a kind of in-house counsel role. It could be all of these things at the same time.

If this is a type of lawyering that appeals to you, there are a few places you might consider working. Some legal organizations specialize in law and organizing. These organizations work in collaboration with independent community organizations and may work with several at the same time. There are also lawyers who are embedded within community organizations, either as single lawyers or as separate legal departments. Being the sole lawyer at a small community organization may not be an ideal first job because you will lack supervision, but it can be a very rewarding job later in your career.

You can expect a law and organizing job to involve less traditional lawyering than other jobs. You may spend some of your time doing organizing or organizing-adjacent work such as attending community meetings or rallies. You will probably spend less time at a desk, and more time in the "field" than almost any other lawyering job. It may require you to become an expert in a number of different areas of law to address the legal needs of the community with which you are working.

Many lawyers who were organizers before law school are drawn to law and organizing, but it is not without its challenges. You may also find yourself in situations where the goals of the community organization running the campaign differ from the goals of the individual client you are representing, causing potential conflicts. Like impact litigation, law and organizing is less client centric than legal services. Unlike impact litigation, though, the focus is on social change not law reform. Your goals will be generated by the community, not by your individual client, and you will pick cases where the client's goals align with the community's goals. Those goals may be fluid, adding to the complexity of this kind of lawyering.

Law and organizing also requires patience. Social movements are not won in a year or sometimes even a lifetime. Because lawyers are subordinate to the community, you will have less control over the outcome and direction of your work. When successful, however, movement lawyering can produce lasting, durable social change that dwarfs anything that can be accomplished in a single lawsuit.

When hiring, organizations want to identify lawyers who are not just parroting support for this model of social change but who will actually feel comfortable practicing it. There is broad skepticism about traditional legal education among people practicing this type of law. Experience working with or for grassroots community organizations is essential to proving that you will be able to defer to the community's goals and objectives and eschew traditional lawyering styles.

Policy/Research

There is another category of organization that does not do litigation and instead focuses exclusively on public policy and/or research. Often people do not think of this work as "practicing law" because you do not need a J.D. to lobby for bills or produce research reports. But while this work does not *require* a J.D., it is a job for which having a law degree provides a clear advantage. These organizations, like impact organizations, are often organized around an issue or set of issues. For example, A Better Balance is a policy organization that focuses on policy issues affecting pregnant persons and women in the workplace. Some of these organizations provide non-legal services to affected populations as well. For example, the Children's Defense Fund engages in policy advocacy and research while also administering literacy programs. Impact organizations may also have policy departments embedded within them. For a public-interest minded lawyer who is not interested in litigation, these organizations might be a good alternative.

There are two sub-categories of policy/research organizations that are worth discussing separately. The first are "think tanks," which are organizations that employ scholars and researchers to produce reports and research on issues of public concern. Some of these organizations, such as the American Enterprise Institute or the Center for American Progress, are considered partisan. Others, such as the Heritage Foundation and the Brookings Institution, are considered ideological even if they are not explicitly aligned with a particular political party. Think tanks tend to have a more general focus than other policy/research organizations. Not everyone who works at these organizations will have law degrees. Indeed, most will probably have advanced graduate degrees or government experience. They represent a bridge between academia, which is often insular and not focused on policy, and advocacy organizations, which may draw on scholarship but do not produce it themselves. An academically-inclined but practice-minded lawyer may enjoy this hybrid experience.

The second sub-category of organization are international human rights organizations. These organizations usually focus on human rights abuses in other countries rather than in the United States, although they may also examine situations in the United States through an international human rights lens. They often produce original research and draft reports that then can be used in advocacy efforts across the globe. They may also engage in that advocacy themselves, or they may pass the baton to local human rights groups to do so.

Law students often start law school interested in international human rights, perhaps because it seems exciting and is more likely to involve foreign travel than other kinds of public interest law. What they often find is that there are fewer human rights jobs than there are people who want such positions, and they are mainly based in a few major cities. Moreover, human rights organizations, especially those abroad, might require long "internships" at no pay before a paid job is even possible to obtain, which is not conducive to paying student loans that many law graduates will have. As a result, the lawyers who end up successfully navigating their way into human rights jobs often are well-off or have other sources of income. These are not necessarily reasons to abandon a desire to do human rights law, but it may be prudent for students considering this path to also get experience in other types of public interest law.

The day-to-day work of a lawyer engaged in policy or research is going to vary greatly depending on the type of policy work or research being done. Lawyers engaged in legislative advocacy may spend most of their time meeting with legislators and coalition partners, drafting proposed legislation, and creating advocacy documents. Lawyers mostly engaged in research may be in the field collecting data themselves, or they may be working independently to analyze data collected by others. Researchers are likely to spend quite a bit of time reading and writing. Though this work can be collaborative, lawyers engaged in policy and research are much less likely to have traditional clients in the way that lawyers engaged in litigation and transactional work have.

Research and policy organizations are looking for a completely different set of skills than organizations who focus on litigation and individual client work. You must learn how to do research and policy advocacy much like you must learn how to do an oral argument or draft a contract. You are unlikely to learn these skills in the law school classroom where the case method reigns supreme. If you want to go into policy or research, you will need to seek out opportunities to learn these skills in elective courses or during your summer internships.

GOVERNMENT

Another category of public interest job is working for the government. This could mean working for a local, state, or the federal government. It could mean working in the executive branch as a government attorney or policy counsel, as a staffer for a member of a legislature, or in the judicial system as a permanent law clerk. Government attorneys engage in litigation, provide legal advice, assist with policymaking, and participate in regulatory systems. The variety of government jobs is practically endless. You will have a very different experience working in a town counsel's office versus working at the Department of Justice versus being a law clerk or congressional staffer.

It is by far the largest category of public interest jobs. More than one in ten law school graduates takes a job in government after graduation.[12] It is more common for lawyers to spend part of their career in government and part of it in the private sector than it is for people to jump back and forth between non-profits and law firms. It may seem like an attractive option. The salaries are slightly higher than at non-profits, and they may be some of the only legal positions that even approach 9 to 5 jobs.

You might ask yourself, though, whether government work is truly public interest lawyering, or whether it is another kind of lawyering entirely. On one hand, our government is supposed to be acting in the public interest, so in a way working for the government is public interest work by definition. On the other hand, we all know that the government does not always act in the public interest, and government lawyers frequently facilitate

---

[12] American Bar Association, Profile of the Legal Profession 132 (2021).

that misconduct. One need only look at the Office of Legal Counsel's memo justifying the CIA's torture program during the Bush Administration to find an example of government lawyers who put their position above principle.[13] Were these lawyers engaged in public interest lawyering simply because they were employed by the government? Most people would say no.

If you want to work for the government, you must be prepared to take positions that you are uncomfortable with. Of course, other public interest attorneys may also find themselves in this position. But I do think there is something unique about working for the government that makes it harder to maintain fealty to your principles than in other contexts. For one thing, every few years the policy preferences of your bosses may change, often resulting in huge swings in the legal positions you are taking. For another, the culture of government work is very different than at non-profits. Lawyers are expected to serve the government's interests whatever they may be, whereas non-profits are more values-based. Public interest organizations are unlikely to require a lawyer to take on a client or cause that they find morally reprehensible as long as that lawyer can participate in other work of the organization. The government asks that of its lawyers all the time. (So, too, do private sector employers, but at least there is no veneer of respectability that comes with supposedly acting in the public interest. Corporate lawyers know they are serving their clients' interests, not the common good).

Finally, because the government has its own institutional interests that often get conflated with the public interest, it's easy to believe that you are working in the public interest simply because that is what the government is supposed to do. That does not mean you cannot be an ethical government lawyer. You can be. But government attorneys have less control over what positions they end up taking and, ultimately, may face more ethical challenges than lawyers practicing in other contexts. Still, the benefits are substantial. A secure job. Decent wages. Reasonable hours. And, if you are lucky, the opportunity to do work on behalf of the people.

---

[13] Andrew Cohen, *The Torture Memos, 10 Years Later*, THE ATLANTIC, Feb. 6, 2012, *available at* https://www.theatlantic.com/national/archive/2012/02/the-torture-memos-10-years-later/252439.

The day-to-day work of a government lawyer will depend on what kind of government lawyer you are. There are government attorneys who spend most of their time in court and others who never see the inside of a courthouse. They run elections. They enforce city codes. They draft government contracts. They write legislation. Knowing you want to work for the government is only the first step in figuring out what you want to do. In any job you are considering, you should make sure you understand what that particular job entails and whether it appeals to you.

The resume of the typical government lawyer is probably more like that of a corporate attorney than the resumes of most other public interest lawyers. The traditional markers of success such as law review are more likely to appear. Importantly, government attorneys are less likely to have taken controversial legal positions in their prior legal jobs. Government agencies want to know that you will be able to handle the unique pressures that government attorneys face that are outlined above. Thus, having strong policy views that are contrary to the prevailing views within the government is seen as a disadvantage.

PUBLIC DEFENDER/ PROSECUTOR OFFICES

Prosecutor and public defender jobs are another option for aspiring public interest lawyers. Although many of these positions are government jobs, they are unique enough to be considered on their own terms. There are quite a few of these jobs nationwide. A county may have just a few civil attorneys but is likely to have a bevy of prosecutors. The Department of Justice employs over 90,000 attorneys, most of whom work in the U.S. Attorney Offices across the country on criminal prosecutions. Some jurisdictions do not have public defender offices and instead rely on private attorneys or non-profits whom the government pays to represent criminal defendants. Regardless of the way they are organized, *Gideon v. Wainwright*, the Supreme Court case that established the right to counsel at the government's expense if you cannot afford an attorney,[14] ensures that there are plenty of jobs representing criminal defendants.

[14] *Gideon v. Wainwright*, 372 U.S. 335 (1963).

Although prosecutors and public defenders both work in the criminal justice system, the two jobs often attract very different people. Many prosecutors see their mission as relatively black and white. They enforce the laws, ensure justice for victims, and hold criminals accountable. They do not have a "client" in the traditional sense of the word. They work for the people.[15] In theory, this means that they are supposed to make decisions based on principles of justice rather than zealously seeking a particular result. In practice, this often does not occur. The adversarial legal system leads prosecutors to adopt an "us vs. them" mentality, and what is right often drops away. A prosecutor may represent the people, but it is not the people who are the prosecutor's proximate influences. Instead, prosecutors often see themselves as representing the interests of law enforcement and see their job as getting a conviction, whatever the cost.

Public defenders play a very different role in the legal system. It is impossible for them to see their work in the same clear-cut way that prosecutors do. For one thing, most of their clients will be guilty of committing a crime, sometimes very serious crimes. Public defenders must hold this truth in their heads while at the same time knowing that even guilty people deserve a defense and that they are playing an important role in our constitutional system. They will often advocate for outcomes that, if they were to succeed, would not be in the public interest. Most public defenders believe the criminal justice system is fundamentally flawed and that their role is to hold the government accountable for abuses and overreach. They have to get used to losing a lot. Most people who go to trial on criminal charges are found guilty. But for public defenders, it is the zealous representation, not the outcome, that motivates them.

The day-to-day work of prosecutors and public defenders is similar in kind if not in substance. Both will spend more time in court than the average lawyer. Both spend much of their other

---

[15] American Bar Association, Criminal Justice Standards for the Prosecution Function, Standard 3-1.2(b), *available at* https://www.americanbar.org/groups/criminal_justice/standards/ProsecutionFunctionFourthEdition (last accessed May 25, 2022) ("The primary duty of the prosecutor is to seek justice within the bounds of the law, not merely to convict. The prosecutor serves the public interest and should act with integrity and balanced judgment. . . .").

time interviewing witnesses, developing case theories, and reviewing evidence. There are differences as well. A public defender will spend a substantial amount of time advising clients, while prosecutors will spend time consulting with law enforcement. Public defenders are more likely to be overburdened and may be forced to take on more clients than they can competently represent. The government is the one who decides when to bring charges, meaning prosecutors often have time to prepare their cases carefully. Public defenders must be reactive and are required to think quickly and nimbly to represent their clients. Both jobs can be stressful, but public defenders are more prone to burnout.

If you are someone who prefers deliberative practice and solitary work, working as either a prosecutor or public defender is probably not the right place for you. If you want to be a trial lawyer, there is no better way to get experience in the courtroom. In either case, you play an important role in the criminal justice system, either by protecting the public or by protecting the rights of criminal defendants.

It is rather uncommon for lawyers to start out as prosecutors and then later become public defenders (though some do go into private criminal defense). Likewise, public defenders are rarely interested in switching sides to become prosecutors. It happens, but for the most part people are drawn to one side or the other and then stick with it. There is also a difference in how people get hired into these jobs. Many prosecutors are hired several years out of law school, while public defender jobs are often advertised to graduating law students.

PRIVATE PUBLIC INTEREST LAW FIRMS

A private public interest law firm is a for-profit firm that makes values-based decisions about what work to do. Their goal is, at least in part, to have a broader social, political, or economic impact on the world. Sometimes these firms are organized around a particular issue like employment discrimination, police misconduct, union organizing, or asylum. They may or may not charge their clients for their services.

Much of this work is possible because of the fee-shifting provisions that exist in many federal statutes, which means that if a plaintiff wins the defendant pays the plaintiff's attorney's fees. Civil rights and employment discrimination are two examples of claims that are subject to fee-shifting statutes. Even if they do charge their clients directly, they may charge less, so-called "low-bono" rates, because their clients may not be wealthy enough to pay full price.

These firms still need to make money so they cannot make decisions solely based on their values. The private public interest law firm's business model will not work if the legal system is not set up to allow lawyers to take on a particular kind of work. A good example of this is eviction defense. There is no fee-shifting statute and your clients may not have money to pay their rent, let alone your fee. Unsurprisingly, I am not aware of any private public interest law firm that does eviction defense.

But when it works, it can represent a lucrative way to practice public interest law. You will make more money at a private public interest law firms than you will at most non-profit organizations, though salaries are still lower than at corporate law firms. For people who want to go into public interest law, but who need to make more money because of family obligations or other financial needs, private public interest law firms can be a good option. It is also easier to transition to other public interest jobs from these firms than it is to transition from a corporate law firm. Non-profit lawyers will respect work done at a private public interest law firm in a way they won't if you chose to work at a corporate law firm. Some public interest lawyers bounce back and forth between non-profits and private public interest law firms throughout their career, something unheard of in the corporate sector.

There are downsides to private public interest law firms. These firms tend to be on the smaller side. That means that like non-profit jobs, there are fewer openings at private public interest law firms than there are at corporate firms. A summer associate position may or may not lead to a permanent position, so you will need to be proactive to get one of these jobs after law school. A good place to start looking is with Harvard Law

School's "Private Public Interest Law and Plaintiff's Firm Guide."[16]

Perhaps the biggest drawback is that these firms need to make a profit, so money must factor into their decisions about what work to do. I would note, however, that you never really get away from this entirely (unless you work for the government). Non-profits also need money to operate. They just get it through fundraising rather than by billing clients. Non-profits often make decisions about what work they do based on what work will allow them to fundraise successfully.

Private public interest law firms are an important part of the public interest ecosystem. There will never be enough non-profits to do all of the important legal work that needs to be done. In fact, we should be encouraging more firms to engage in values-based lawyering. For young lawyers, private public interest law firms can represent a rare opportunity to practice public interest law while earning a higher-than-average public interest salary.

ACADEMIA

Law teaching is not an obvious career choice for aspiring public interest lawyers, but you can find ways to practice public interest law in academia. There are different kinds of professors teaching at law schools. Doctrinal professors teach lecture and seminar courses and spend most of the rest of their time engaged in scholarship. Clinical professors teach law school clinics and other experiential courses. They may or may not teach other classes or do research. At some schools, there is also a third kind of professor who teaches legal writing. These professors play different roles in the law school ecosystem. Each job presents different opportunities for practicing public interest law.

It is relatively easy for clinical professors to practice public interest law. Most law school clinics provide pro bono legal services to clients and many do work that is properly classified as public interest law. Most clinical professors come from practice and a good number of them were public interest lawyers

---

[16] Harvard Law School, Private Public Interest Law and Plaintiff's Firm Guide, https://hls.harvard.edu/dept/opia/private-public-interest-law-and-plaintiffs-firm-guide (last accessed on May 18, 2022).

before going into teaching. There are many advantages to practicing public interest law in a law school setting. You have a more flexible schedule and more control over your docket than many lawyers. Clinical professors are entitled to academic freedom at most schools and may enjoy a form of job security even if it is not considered traditional "tenure." They also need to worry less about fundraising because the law school is paying their salary, which tends to be higher than in the non-profit sector.

There are also relatively few of these jobs and consequently, they are hard to get. Clinical teaching candidates have in recent years been required to meet many of the same requirements as doctrinal candidates: a degree from a top-ranked law school, a clerkship, and at least some passing interest in scholarship. A good resource for finding clinical teaching opportunities is the Clinical Legal Education Association job board.[17]

The day-to-day job of a clinical professor will involve some legal practice, some teaching, and sometimes scholarship as well. A clinical professor typically teaches in the classroom and teaches the fieldwork component of the course.

It is much harder to use a doctrinal teaching position to practice public interest law, though not impossible. The first difficulty is that your job does not require any practice of law whatsoever. Moreover, doctrinal faculty must spend much of their time producing scholarship, which limits the time available for anything else. At some schools, active engagement in the practice of law is frowned upon and actively discouraged.

After tenure, however, doctrinal professors have much more freedom to decide how to spend their time and many decide to spend at least part of that time engaging in what I would call public interest lawyering. A good example of this is Elizabeth Warren, who before her Senate run, was a tenured law professor at Harvard Law School. During her time at Harvard, Warren spent years advocating for bankruptcy reform among other advocacy work.[18] Her research was intimately connected with

---

[17] Clinical Legal Education Association, Jobs, *available at* https://www.cleaweb.org/Jobs (last accessed May 19, 2022).

[18] Sharon Cohen, *Elizabeth Warren's Rise Started by Looking at the Bottom*, ASSOCIATED PRESS, Aug. 25, 2019, available at https://apnews.com/article/elizabeth-

this work. Many professors represent clients on a pro bono basis or are active on an issue or set of issues. Because of their platform, they can really make a difference.

It would be a stretch to say that doctrinal professors are public interest lawyers, however. Any public interest lawyering is incidental to their main job, which is teaching law students and producing research. The salary they collect for doing this work allows them the freedom to spend a portion of their time doing other things. But it may be ten years or more into their career before they have the freedom to do so. The bottom line is that if you want to be a legal academic, you can also—with enough planning—do some public interest lawyering. But I would not suggest that you become a doctrinal law professor in order to engage in public interesting lawyering. There are many other career paths that make more sense if that is your ultimate goal.

The day-to-day job of a doctrinal professor will involve more time in the classroom and more time on research, with any public interest lawyering filling in the margins. Doctrinal teaching might make sense for a lawyer who likes the university environment and who wants to engage in scholarship and teaching in addition to or instead of traditional legal practice.

It may be hardest for legal writing professors to practice public interest law. They often enjoy less status and job security and have a higher teaching load than either clinical professors or doctrinal professors. Their job, while important and valuable, is not conducive to outside pro bono work. They spend endless hours editing and commenting on memos and briefs written by first-year law students. There is not much time left for them to do anything else.

How to land a job in academia is outside the scope of this book, but there are many resources available if this is a career path that interests you. For an overview of how to get a doctrinal teaching position, you can read Yale Law School's guide for

---

warren-financial-markets-ap-top-news-courts-chicago-8bbb0cbe763a407db4a9b5d56 3dc56ca.

Preparing for a Career in Law Teaching.[19] For those interested in clinical teaching, Professor Claudia Flores has an excellent blog post entitled "How to Become a Clinical Law Professor."[20]

PRIVATE COMPANIES

Another kind of job that might appeal to an aspiring public interest lawyer is working for a private company that is engaged in social entrepreneurship, which is the idea that private companies can pursue profits while also contributing to the public good.[21] In order to qualify as a public interest job, more than a nominal contribution to the public good is required. For example, a company that donates a small portion of its profits to charity, without more, would not fit my definition of social entrepreneurship. Instead, the term describes companies who exist primarily to make the world a better place, even if they try to make some money along the way.

Like all kinds of public interest lawyering, there are pros and cons to going this route. The pros are apparent—in most cases, private companies will pay more than non-profits or government. If your position comes with stock options or other profit-sharing agreements, you could make a lot more. Being a social entrepreneur also allows you to be more creative than you can often be when taking on traditional lawyering roles. It allows you to try to solve problems in innovative ways, creating something new rather than simply following old playbooks of others before you.

Because these companies tend to be small, the lawyers who work for them may be asked to take on a variety of legal and non-legal roles. For that reason, these jobs might appeal to lawyers who are less keen on litigating or lawyering in general. They allow lawyers to use their legal training in a way that doesn't always look like traditional lawyering. If you want to be

---

[19] Yale Law School, Preparing for a Job in Law Teaching, https://law.yale.edu/studying-law-yale/areas-interest/law-teaching/law-teaching-program/preparing-career-law-teaching (last accessed on May 25, 2022).

[20] Claudia Flores, *How to Become a Clinical Law Professor*, SUMMARY, JUDGMENT, June 25, 2020, *available at* https://www.summarycommajudgment.com/blog/how-to-become-a-clinical-law-professor.

[21] U.S. Chamber of Commerce, What is a Social Entrepreneur?, https://www.uschamber.com/co/start/startup/what-is-social-entrepreneurship (last accessed May 25, 2022).

a public interest lawyer but feel that your skillset is well suited for business, this could a path for you.

The most obvious downside is that when you are working for a private company, it is difficult not to let profits drive your decision-making and there is always the danger that your commitment to the public good will melt away when profits are on the line. Moreover, even a limited commitment to profits could restrict the amount of good you can do. When you try to serve two masters, one often gets the short end of the stick. In business, profits tend to win out over principles. Social entrepreneurship also requires a certain tolerance of risk that many lawyers do not have. Start-ups fail and companies go bankrupt. Ideas that seem good sometimes don't pan out. Sure, non-profits and law firms can also go under, but they usually don't. Businesses fail all the time.

Another disadvantage is that unlike other types of public interest jobs, there is no clear pipeline from law school into these positions. Getting one may require spending a few years getting experience and then a few more pounding the pavement looking for a good fit. Lawyers who went to work at a law firm after graduation may find it easier to transition to a public interest job at a private company than to go into the non-profit world. In fact, having corporate experience may give you an advantage over traditional public interest lawyers when applying for these jobs.

CHAPTER 3

BEFORE LAW SCHOOL

Unlike in many countries, law is not typically taught as an undergraduate degree in the United States. Most lawyers in the U.S. spent four years studying something other than law before they went to law school. They might have also spent a few years after college working before returning to law school. Sixty-five percent of law students take some time off between their undergraduate degree and law school.[1]

These are precious years. Once you are a lawyer, you will probably be a lawyer for the rest of your life. Even if you do not practice law, other people will treat you like a lawyer and expect you to use your legal skills in whatever role you take on. This is no less true for aspiring public interest lawyers. You will be a better lawyer later if you spend these years before law school developing other academic and professional skills that you can rely on to supplement your legal education.

It is during these years that many students begin thinking about public interest law as a possible career path, perhaps after becoming passionate about social or political issues in college or after getting some job experience after college in an adjacent field. Although you do not need to be planning for law school the moment you graduate from high school, there are certain steps you can take that will make your path to law school smoother.

THE COLLEGE YEARS

You may arrive at college with very little idea of what you want to do. During your first year or two, you will be encouraged to experiment and explore. By the end of your second year, however, most colleges and universities expect you to pick a major, which requires at least some forethought about what you want to do after graduation. For some career paths, such as becoming a doctor, what you major in is critical. If you do not major in a pre-med subject and then later decide to go to medical

[1] American Bar Association, Profile of the Legal Profession 54 (2021).

school, you may need to do an extra year of school so you can take the necessary prerequisites.

This is not the case for law school. You can major in anything under the sun and still go to law school after you graduate. You should not feel like you need to pick a "pre-law" undergraduate major like legal studies or political science. The time before law school should be an opportunity for you to get a well-rounded education. Law school is full of students who were English literature, psychology, and biology majors. One overlooked major is philosophy, which allows you to learn analytic reasoning and persuasion while still getting a well-rounded liberal arts education. You may find your undergraduate degree helpful in whatever area of law you end up practicing. Many science and engineering students go on to become patent lawyers, for example. A degree in critical race studies might start you on a path to practicing civil rights law. But your undergraduate major could also end up being completely unrelated to your legal career. Three years in law school is more than enough time to learn everything you need to know.

I would steer away from the undergraduate degrees in law that have begun popping up around the country. These programs are usually located within law schools with courses taught by law professors. Often the courses are slightly dumbed-down versions of the classes that law students take their first year of law school. No one needs to take the first year of law school twice. You will be adding little to your legal education and you will be missing out on an opportunity that you will never get back to study something else. Take advantage of the freedom of being able to follow your interests. I guarantee it will only make you a better lawyer later.

Having a liberal arts undergraduate major will not negatively affect your chances of getting into a good law school. In fact, quite the opposite is true. Law school admissions committees are looking for good grades and high LSAT scores. But they are also looking for prospective students who are interesting, well rounded, and passionate.

When picking electives, you may decide to take a few courses that are more closely related to law. For example, I have had many students who took an undergraduate course in constitutional law and found it a formative class that solidified their desire to go to law school. If you find yourself drawn to a particular social issue, you may take a class or two to learn about it. The reason to take these courses as electives is not to gain a credential, but to work out whether law school is the right path for you and to nurture your passions. You do not need to major in these fields to accomplish those goals.

Some of the most useful courses you can take are foreign language classes. If you can leave college with proficiency in a language, particularly one that is spoken widely in the United States, you will reap the rewards later in your legal career. Speaking a second language is useful for all lawyers, but it is particularly useful for public interest lawyers who may work at organizations that don't have the resources to hire translators and who are more likely to represent people who do not speak English. Moreover, you may never have time to master a language again, particularly after entering law practice.

If you are undecided about which language to study, pick Spanish. It is the second most common language in the United States and you will undoubtedly have clients who speak it. If you know which city or state you want to practice in after you graduate from law school, you can look up common languages spoken in that state. Mandarin, for example, is the third most common language after English and Spanish in New York, whereas it is Haitian creole in Florida, and Korean in Alabama.[2] The important thing is to pick a language that you will actually use.

You will also need to decide how to spend your time out of the classroom in college, and this is where an aspiring public interest lawyer may want to make different decisions than other students interested in law school. As I talk about later in the book, proving your passion for public interest work turns out to be one of the most important things you can do to maximize your chances of getting a public interest job. Although you are not required to do so, beginning to build up your resume before law school can be helpful for getting your first internship, which in

---

[2] America as a multilingual nation, Language Log, available at https://languagelog.ldc.upenn.edu/nll/?p=45885 (last accessed May 19, 2022).

turn will be useful for getting your second internship, your first job, and so on. This could take the form of volunteering, student organizations, or a semester abroad. It could also be a law-related internship. Many public interest organizations hire college interns.

However, you should choose activities that you enjoy for their own sake, not just because of how they look on your resume. Your lack of interest will be transparent to anyone who digs any deeper than a quick glance at your resume. Moreover, it is better to choose a few activities that you devote more time to rather than many activities where your involvement is only superficial. If you have too many activities on your resume, people will assume your involvement was trivial, even when it was not. They key here is that you are developing your own interest and passions, not ticking boxes.

AFTER COLLEGE

It is a good idea to spend a few years working after college before going to law school. The first reason is strategic: you will be a better law school candidate a few years out of school than you will be your senior year of college.

The second reason is more personal. Unlike in the medical profession, it only takes three years of professional training to become a lawyer. There is no reason you need to start your legal career at 25 as opposed to 27 or 28. Use those years between college and law school to get some real-world experience and figure out what you really want to do. You will get more out of law school if you take a few years off. The experiences you gain will be helpful in your future legal career.

Most people must work during these years to support themselves. If this is you, try to work in at least one job that is law adjacent. It will help you get a clearer sense of why you want to go to law school and what you want to do with your degree. For example, working as a paralegal might help you decide that law school is right for you. You may also realize that you do not want to be a lawyer. And wouldn't it be great to learn that before taking on massive quantities of debt?

Perhaps even more important than getting law-adjacent experience, however, is thinking through what kinds of job experiences are likely to make you an attractive law school applicant and candidate for public interest scholarships. Going to work at an investment bank may seem like a prestigious job to get out of college, but no one is going to look at it and see a future public interest lawyer. Working at a preschool may be God's work, but it will not earn you a public interest scholarship. If you are in doubt, try to imagine what will give you material to write a compelling admission essay. If it's hard for you to imagine, then the admissions committee is not going to see it either. When in doubt, pick something that has a public service component.

Some people decide to get a master's degree, even if they know they eventually intend to go on to law school. If you are able to get a master's degree without taking on debt (either because you receive a scholarship or it is a funded program), then it is not a bad way to spend two years. If you have to take on debt, though, I would counsel against it. You do not need a master's degree to practice law and it is unlikely to give you much of an advantage in the job market. If you want to be a public interest lawyer, you will want to do everything you can to keep your debt manageable. The cost-benefit analysis of an expensive master's degree simply does not come out in your favor.

Even if you decide to get a master's degree, you should still try to work for at least one year before going to law school. Even minimal time in the job market as a non-lawyer is an important experience that you will never be able to get again.

HOW TO DECIDE IF LAW SCHOOL IS RIGHT FOR YOU

Before you apply to law school, you will want to think long and hard about whether law school is right for you. The reason is simple: it is a very expensive wrong choice. Law school costs hundreds of thousands of dollars. Even if you decide after law school that you do not want to practice law, your student debt may force you to. You do not want to get trapped in a profession that makes you unhappy.

Many college students decide to go to law school as a kind of default. They are not good at science and math, so medical school is out. Their interests are not developed or strong enough to apply to PhD programs. Business school is an option, but most people get an MBA after working for a few years, not straight out of college. For students who want to go to graduate school that leaves law school, which is seen as a kind of general graduate degree that gives you lots of options.

The problem with this is that a J.D. is not a general degree. Law schools are professional schools. They train *lawyers.* If you do not want to be a lawyer, think long and hard about whether to go to law school. It is true that a law degree can be helpful in other fields. Many law graduates go into business, for example. But there are easier pathways into those jobs that do not require taking on hundreds of thousands of dollars in debt. If you do not want to be a lawyer but believe that a law degree is essential to what you want to do, go talk to people in the field to see if there is an easier way. There probably is.

Public interest students are more prone to making this mistake than most. For students with a general desire to make a difference in the world or to help people, law school can seem like an attractive option. But these students should be particularly careful about taking on law school debt because many of the other alternatives careers available to them—jobs that will allow them to help people—will not pay enough to pay off law school loans. Jobs such as social work, teaching, organizing, and journalism (to name a few professions that may attract public interest-minded students) all pay substantially less than public interest law jobs. Moreover, many law school loan repayment programs, which allow some public interest lawyers to get a break on their student loans, do not cover graduates in non-legal jobs.

So how do you know if law school is right for you? The easiest way to figure it out is to either work in a law adjacent job after college or, if that does not fit in with your life plans, talk to as many lawyers as possible. Even lawyers who love their jobs are usually pretty frank about the downsides of being a lawyer. They will be able to give you guidance on whether law school is right for you.

You may also want to take a peek at the courses offered by the law schools you are considering. If few or none of the classes sound interesting, then law school is probably not for you. The one caveat to this advice is that the first-year curriculum at most law schools is not geared towards public interest students. You will need to look past the first year at electives, seminars, and experiential courses to really determine whether there will be classes that interest you.

APPLYING TO LAW SCHOOL

For better or worse, the legal profession is very focused on status, prestige, and credentialing. The law school you attend matters. This is true whether you want to work for the U.S. government, a big law firm, or a public interest organization. In general, the higher ranked your law school is, the more opportunities you will have after law school, including in public interest law. The rankings that almost everyone uses are those published each year by U.S. News and World Report.[3] Everyone recognizes that these rankings are flawed, but that does not stop employers from making hiring decisions based on them.

The two most important factors that determine which law schools will offer you admission are your undergraduate grade point average (GPA) and your LSAT score. To put yourself in the absolute best position to get into the highest ranked law school as possible, you should focus on these two things. Schools will also use these metrics to dole out financial aid and scholarships, which are particularly important for public interest students expecting lower salaries upon graduation.

GPA is self-explanatory—law schools expect you to get high grades, a 3.5 GPA or higher for most mid-ranked law schools and a 3.8 or higher for the top law schools. If you are not a good student in college, you will need to find another career. Law school will not be an option.

For many students, the LSAT is the most stressful part of the law school admissions process. In recent years, some law schools have moved away from the LSAT by either accepting the GRE instead or by making any standardized test optional. Recently, a committee of the American Bar Association

[3] U.S. News and World Report 2023 Law School Rankings, available at https://www.usnews.com/best-graduate-schools/top-law-schools/law-rankings (last accessed on May 19, 2022).

recommended that the ABA remove the "valid and reliable admissions test" requirement for accreditation.[4] Perhaps in the future the LSAT will fade away as an important component of a law school application. Until then, however, you should plan on taking the LSAT to avoid the implication that you would have done poorly on the test. Moreover, you will want to do well. "Well" is relative, but in general, you should aim for at least the median LSAT score of the schools you wish to attend. For people who excel at standardized tests, it may be a piece of cake to do well on the LSAT. For others, it is easier said than done. Plan on devoting as much time as it will take to get the best score you can. If you are working or going to school fulltime, it can be hard to find time to study. You have to find the time anyway.

The LSAT is important because it affects where you go to law school, which in turn affects your career opportunities after law school. Because of this, if you take the LSAT and do poorly, you may want to delay law school for a year so that you can take the LSAT again. There is no rush to go to law school, and you want to give yourself the best chance to succeed. If you have the financial resources to do so, you should take a course or engage a private tutor. People who try to study for the LSAT on the cheap are cheating themselves. This is not the place to save money. It is worth the expense. If you cannot afford to pay for LSAT preparation, try to take advantage of the free resources that are available. Some LSAT prep programs have free resources available for underprivileged law school applicants.[5]

If you do all of that and you are not happy with your score, it is not the end of the world. Many successful lawyers had average LSAT scores and have done just fine. In my experience, it is easier to overcome a bad LSAT score than it is a low GPA. You will just need to rely on other parts of the application, such

---

[4] American Bar Association, Recommended Revisions to Standards 501 and 503 for Council Approval for Notice and Comment 1 (2022), available at https://www.americanbar.org/content/dam/aba/administrative/legal_education_and_admissions_to_the_bar/council_reports_and_resolutions/may22/22-may-memo-revisions-501-503.pdf.

[5] *See, e.g.*, SEO Law Catalyst, https://www.seo-usa.org/law/our-program/catalyst (last accessed May 25, 2022); LSAC Plus Program, https://www.lsac.org/discover-law/diversity-law-school/prelaw-undergraduate-scholars-plus-programs (last accessed May 25, 2022).

as grades, extracurricular activities, and job experience. It can be done. It will just be harder.

The other thing you can do to maximize your success in the law school application process is to learn how to tell a compelling story about yourself. If your GPA or LSAT score is mediocre then this storytelling will be doubly important. It is here that aspiring public interest lawyers have an advantage. Many people go to law school to make a lot of money, but that does not make a very good admissions essay. So most people will focus on the fact that they want to use their law degree for good or that they want to help people, even if that's not the real reason they want to go to law school. Aspiring public interest lawyers are at an advantage because that story will be true.

What makes a compelling story? In short, you want to convince the reader that your whole life up to this point has led you to the conclusion that you want to do *x* and the way that you will do *x* is by becoming a lawyer. It doesn't matter if your story is more complicated than that. Everyone's story is. But when you are telling your story in an admissions essay, all nuance needs to be stripped away. Every moment of your life has been leading up to this moment. This is one reason why extracurricular activities that are in line with your passions can be helpful in telling a compelling story. So too are personal experiences that have led you to the path you are on today. The story you tell does not have to be the only story you could tell. In fact, you will probably tell many different versions of your story throughout your life. It just needs to be one of the true versions.

CHOOSING A LAW SCHOOL

You have decided that you want to go to law school, you have taken the LSAT, and now you need to figure out where to apply and, if you have options, which law school to attend. The general answer will not be a surprise if you have read up to this point: all else being equal a higher-ranked school will be a better bet than a lower-ranked school. But of course, things are never equal. Here are some of the additional factors you might want to consider that could cause you to deviate from the general advice to go to the highest-ranked school you get into.

Specialized Curriculum

Some schools may be particularly strong in a certain sub-field that you are interested in and you may wonder whether this should be a deciding factor for which law school you choose. For example, Lewis and Clark Law School has a top-ranked environmental program, and you may be interested in going there if you want to practice environmental law after law school. So should you go to a lower-ranked law school if it has strong program in a sub-field you are interested in?

Maybe. If two schools are in the same tier, then it might make sense to choose the school with the more highly-regarded program in the sub-specialty that you are interested in. But the more difference there is between the rankings of the two schools, the less likely it is to make sense to go with the lower-ranked school, regardless of what programs are available there.

Law school is not like graduate school where it is very important to have someone on the faculty that specializes in your particular sub-field of academic study. For PhD students, it may be impossible to graduate without that institutional support because you will not have an advisor who is interested in your research and committed to helping you succeed.

Law school is different. You could not take a single environmental law course in law school and you could still go on to have a successful career in environmental justice with the right summer internships and extracurricular activities. You could start a student group that pairs students with volunteer opportunities in environmental law. You could organize a symposium through law review on an environmental law topic. You could write a major research paper on some environmental law topic. And you could do all of this without a single person on the faculty that knows anything about environmental law.

It is better to go to a school that has a strong program in whatever area of law you are interested in, but it may not be worth giving up the benefit of going to a higher-ranked school.

Public Interest Programs

Some schools have more of a focus on public interest than your average school. For example, the City University of New

York (CUNY) School of Law is well known in public interest circles for having a strong focus on public interest law. I have talked to many students who have gone to CUNY over better-ranked New York schools for that reason. So if you have a choice, should you choose a school that has a better public interest program?

This is a tougher question to answer than whether specialized curriculum matters. Even at schools with a strong focus on public interest, there will be immense pressure to abandon that path and go work for a law firm. If you do not have institutional support to forge a public interest career, it can be difficult to resist the temptation of six-figure law firm salaries. You could still get the experience you need to get a public interest job after graduation. Few schools have no public interest opportunities. But if the school does not prioritize public interest work, you may find it hard to stay focused on your goals.

I would ask yourself how self motivated you are. If you think you will stay focused on your goals regardless of what message you get from your school or your classmates, then go to the higher-ranked school. But if you feel like you will need that institutional support, a strong public interest program may be more important to your decision. And, as with specialized curricula, a strong public interest program should be less of a factor the greater the difference is between the ranking of the two schools.

One additional factor to consider is what kind of public interest job you want. For some public interest jobs, going to a school with a strong public interest program may be all you need to get the job you want. Some legal aid and state public defender offices fall into this category. For other public interest jobs, going to a highly-ranked school is more important that almost anything else. For instance, if you want to get a job at one of the top impact litigation organizations or best private public law firms, a degree from a top school is a must. If you do not know which category your goal job falls into, ask people with that job now.

It may be difficult to figure out at a glance which schools have strong public interest programs. As I explain below, all law schools want you to think that they care about public interest law. If you can, talk to current and recently graduated students from the schools you are considering to figure out what is a real commitment to public interest and what is just marketing.

Geography

Let's say that you are from St. Louis and you want to move back there after graduation. The two schools you are choosing between are St. Louis University, a mid-ranked local school, and Emory University, a better-ranked law school in Atlanta, a place you have no interest in living after graduation. Which law school should you chose? How much does geography matter?

It is more important than you might think. With the exception of a handful of "national" law schools, most law graduates will go on to work in the region, if not the city, where they went to law school. Some of this is because many law students choose law schools close to home. But some of it is because you will have a much easier time getting a job near where you went to law school. The school and your professors will have more connections, there will be more alumni in the area wanting to hire graduates from your school, and you will know more people through your extracurricular activities or networking opportunities at your school.

When I taught at the University at Buffalo School of Law, I met many students who had come from elsewhere and had plans to move back. I also met students from upstate New York who wanted to leave as soon as they graduated and never come back. Most of those people ended up in Buffalo. It was just easier for them to get a job in Buffalo than elsewhere. This is even true to some extent for the top law schools. If you have a choice between Stanford and Harvard and you want to end up in San Francisco, you should probably go to Stanford. Regional advantage matters.

Does that mean that it is impossible to move elsewhere after graduating? No, especially if you move your time horizon out. I have a friend from Colorado who went to Washington University in St. Louis. He applied to some jobs in Colorado but ended up taking a (very good) job in St. Louis. A decade later, he made the move back to Colorado. At that point, it didn't matter as much where he went to law school because he was applying based on his experience and reputation.

You should consider geography in deciding where to go to law school. Ranking matters too, but geography matters more than people think.

Financial Aid

Financial aid is probably the hardest factor to discuss because everyone's financial circumstances are so different. That said, there are a few things worth discussing that apply to almost anyone. First, you may think that if you are planning on going into public interest, you should be very concerned about the amount of loans you must take out. But this is not always the case. Instead, you should look both at what you need to borrow initially and how much you will ultimately need to pay off.

Some schools provide scholarships up front to students they want to lure away from better law schools. Other law schools, including many of the highest ranked law schools, do not discount tuition much on the front end, but offer a loan repayment plan to graduates who take certain kinds of public interest jobs. These loan repayment programs mean that it may be cheaper in the end to go to a more expensive school that has a good loan repayment program.

There are a few caveats to this advice. First, if you are considering a school that has a loan repayment program, you will want to dig into the details of the program to make sure that it will apply to the work you want to do after law school. Some schools' programs do not extend to all kinds of public interest work. If you want to go be a public defender, for example, but your school's repayment program does not count criminal defense work as a qualifying public interest job, you need to know that before you decide to go there. Few, if any, programs repay loans for graduates working at private public interest law firms or for private companies, regardless of whether you are doing public interest work. And you will want to read the fine print to see how much of your loans the program will actually pay. Some programs are more generous than others. Finally, many schools do not have a loan repayment program at all. You should be taking these programs into account when evaluating financial aid as a factor in your decision

A good place to start is the American Bar Association's guide to law school loan repayment programs.[6] Then talk to the financial aid offices of the schools you are considering. They are the experts in the loan repayment programs their schools offer. Finally, ask to speak to graduates who are enrolled in the loan repayment program to see whether the reality lives up to the promise. That will allow you to make a decision based on the actual cost to you of going to a particular school instead of the sticker price.

If the school you are considering does not have a loan repayment program, there still may be ways to make it work financially. Even law schools without merit-based scholarships still award need-based aid. If you are unhappy with the first financial aid package you receive, go back to the financial aid office and ask if they can increase your aid. Especially if you are deciding between two similarly-ranked law schools, the financial aid office may be willing to work with you.

There is also a federal loan forgiveness program for people who work in qualifying public interest jobs for ten years after graduation.[7] When the program first rolled out it seemed promising, but after a few years many people began to complain that minor technicalities were preventing them from having their loans forgiven. Some people tried to comply with the program for years before being told their loans were no longer eligible for forgiveness. In the past year, however, the Department of Education has made some changes to the program that have allowed many more people to get the loan forgiveness they were promised. No one knows what will happen to the program in the future. In other words, the federal program may be an option, but you should have a backup plan in case the program changes.

Finally, while outside scholarships are less common for law school, they do exist. For example, Soros New Americans Fellowship pays for first- and second-generation Americans to

---

[6] American Bar Association, Loan Repayment Assistance Programs, https://www.americanbar.org/groups/center-pro-bono/resources/directory_of_law_school_public_interest_pro_bono_programs/definitions/pi_lrap.

[7] Federal Student Aid, Federal Service Loan Forgiveness, https://studentaid.gov/manage-loans/forgiveness-cancellation/public-service.

get graduate degrees.[8] The Marshall-Motley Scholars Program run by the NAACP allows future civil rights lawyers from the South to go to law school tuition free if they commit to working in public interest for 8 years after graduation.[9] These scholarships are worth applying for even if they are hard to get.

After you have exhausted all funding sources, try to minimize how many loans you have to take out. Do not take out more money than you need during law school. You should not be living like royalty. Each dollar you take out today in loans will cost you much more later.

Once you know how much in loans you will need to take out (and how much will be forgiven later), you should figure out what your monthly payment will be. If the 10-year repayment plan results in a monthly payment that is too high, consider extending your repayment period to 15 or 20 years. You may be hesitant to do this, but people regularly take out 30-year mortgages. As long as you are paying off your loans, it does not matter if you pay them back slowly. But you simply must calculate this monthly payment. Surprisingly, many students never do and just assume that they will not be able to afford to live on a public interest salary. Before coming to that conclusion, you should at least do the math.

If you do all of these things, you will likely discover that your loan payments are manageable on a public interest salary. Even entry-level public interest jobs pay more than equivalent non-legal jobs, because organizations must offer a higher salary to attract good candidates (many of whom have student loans to pay). Moreover, your salary will only rise over time. You will get raises and may be able to transition into a better-paid job after a few years. Even if your budget is a little tight for a few years, you want to think about your long-term earning potential when deciding whether to follow a particular career path.

If you determine that even using all of these strategies, you will not be able to afford to take a public interest job, then you should think seriously about whether you want to go to law

---

8 Paul & Daisy Soros Fellowship for New Americans, https://www.pdsoros.org (last accessed May 20, 2022).

9 Legal Defense Fund Marshall-Motley Scholar Program, https://marshallmotleyscholars.org (last accessed May 20, 2022).

school at all (or whether to apply again in another cycle with a better LSAT score to schools with better loan repayment programs). If the amount of loans you must take out means you have to take a job you do not want, then you should ask yourself whether it is worth it.

CHAPTER 4

LAW SCHOOL

The three years of law school are some of the most formative of a young lawyer's professional life. The decisions that you make during these years set the trajectory of your career.

HOW YOU SHOULD SPEND YOUR TIME IN LAW SCHOOL

Law school may seem endless while you are there, but three years is not a lot of time to do everything you need to do to get a public interest job after law school. There are, of course, differences in what you need to do depending on what kind of public interest job you want. For any job you want, however, the three most important ways you can spend your time in law school are by getting experience, proving your passion, and making connections.

Getting Experience

The most important thing you can do as an aspiring public interest lawyer is get real legal experience. It used to be possible to graduate from law school without ever having done any real legal work. That is less true now—the American Bar Association now requires six experiential credits to graduate from ABA-accredited law schools[1]—but you should still work to get as much experience as possible.

The reason is simple: public interest organizations cannot afford to hire attorneys that are not "practice ready." They may only hire one or two attorneys a year depending on the size of the organization, and most work on lean budgets that don't leave room for dead weight. When hiring, they are looking for attorneys who have the experience to start contributing immediately. That puts new lawyers at a disadvantage, but you can mitigate this disadvantage by getting as much experience as possible in law school.

---

[1] American Bar Association, Standards and Rules of Procedure for Approval of Law Schools, Standard 303(a)(3) (2021).

Even for public interest employers who are not as cash strapped as non-profit organizations–like government and private sector employers–having relevant experience on your resume is an advantage. There will be someone else applying who has directly applicable experience. You do not want to have to explain why they should hire you instead.

What you are looking for here is not just lines on your resume, but actual experiences you can talk about in a cover letter or job interview. When choosing summer internships, you should look for organizations that won't just lock you in a room and ask you to write research memos all summer. Instead, you should look for an internship that will give you a wide range of experiences that better approximates the work that lawyers actually do, such as client meetings and court appearances.

You can also get experience during the school year. Law school clinics permit second- and third-year law students to practice under limited law licenses and usually provide students with much more substantive experiences than summer internships. You should enroll in a clinic as soon as possible and for as long as possible. Take more than one clinic if you can. Even in your first year, there are sometimes volunteer opportunities that will allow you to get your feet wet.

Ideally, you would tailor the experience you get in law school to the work you want to do afterwards, though this is more important for some kinds of public interest jobs than others. Government agencies may care less about whether you have previous government experience than public interest organizations, for example. When in doubt, you can ask lawyers currently doing the job you want what kind of experience you should aim to get in law school. They will know.

Some experiences may be counterproductive depending on your career goals. If you want to be a public defender, doing a prosecution externship is probably going to be seen as a mark against you. If you want to be a workers' rights attorney, don't go work for a union-busting law firm. You might not want to volunteer in the legal department of a radical political group if you want to go work for the federal government. You might think it would be useful to get experience doing work "on the other side," but much of the time, it just causes potential employers to doubt you are a good fit.

Proving Your Passion

When someone looks at your resume, they should think: "That person is going to be a public interest lawyer." It should be clear that you are dedicated to the project of making the world a better place. If you want to have a public interest career, you need to prove to the gatekeepers of the profession—fellowship committees and hiring committees—that you really want it. And showing is always easier than telling.

Many students interested in public interest law decide to spend their second summer at a law firm. They may be curious about what it is like to work at a law firm, or they may want to make money to pay down some of their student loans. Whatever the reason, these students assume that a summer at a law firm won't affect their public interest job prospects that much and maybe that it will make them look well-rounded.

But this is not how it works at all. Getting a public interest job is hard, much harder in many cases than getting a law firm job. A public interest organization will have many applicants to choose from. These organizations are looking for applicants who have the experience they need to hit the ground running, but they are also looking for applicants who can prove that they are dedicated to public interest law. A summer at a law firm signals the opposite. You can argue that you are passionate about public interest law until you are blue in the face, but your resume will speak for itself.

Public interest organizations cannot afford to hire someone whose heart is not in the work. Being a public interest lawyer is hard and no one is doing it for the money. You have to care about it if you are going to succeed. Because anyone can feign interest in an interview, organizations look at your resume as a proxy for your passion.

Is it impossible to spend a summer at a law firm and then get a public interest job? No, but it will make it harder. I have been on hiring committees where applicants were rejected solely because they summered at a law firm. It was an easy way to reject people. There are other ways to prove your passion to potential employers. Your experience before law school and your activities and courses during the school year will help. But the strongest signal to public interest organization will be what you do that second summer.

So how do you prove your passion? It's simple: make decisions like someone who is committed to public interest.

Making Connections and Finding Mentors

Connections matter in public interest law just like they do everywhere else. One reason to spend your summers in law school at two different public interest organizations is that you will make more connections that way. If you are lucky, you may end up working at one of those organizations. Even if you do not, you'll have people there who can serve as recommenders or who can put in a good word for you with their friends. You can also make connections during the school year. Many schools invite public interest lawyers to campus to give talks. You should attend and stay after to meet them individually. Get to know professors who have connections in the public interest world too. As painful as it may be to do this kind of "networking," you have to do it.

In addition, you should not overlook how important making connections with other law students is. In law school, they are just as clueless and confused as you are. They certainly do not hold the keys to jobs you want. But there are several ways connections with your law school classmates can reap professional dividends in the long run. First, while they may not be able to get you a job, they might know someone who can. Even a reference from a fellow classmate might make the difference between getting an interview and getting a rejection letter. Second, your classmates will not always be on the low rung of the career ladder. In just a few years, they will start their own careers and may end up in a position to help you down the line. Conversely, it is a bad idea to antagonize your classmates. The reputation you develop in law school does not evaporate on graduation day.

One of the most important things you can do as an aspiring public interest lawyer is to find mentors to help you along the way. But finding a mentor is easier said than done. How do you find a mentor? And perhaps more importantly, how do you find a *good* mentor?

There are different kinds of mentors and you should try to find at least one of each. There are mentors who are at an advanced stage in their career and who can help you make the connections you need to succeed. These are *rainmaker* mentors. There are also mentors who are just a few years ahead of you in their careers who can provide a more personal kind of mentorship. These are *confidant* mentors. Each of these mentors fulfills a different role in your professional development.

Rainmaker mentors are important because they can open doors for you. They are likely to have a wide network of connections, and if they believe in you, they can give you access to their network. The rainmaker mentor can also provide advice, but it tends to be the 10,000-foot kind. It has been a while since they were in your shoes. They are going to be much better at dispensing advice about the overall trajectory of your career than about a particular fellowship that may not have existed when they were applying or about a clerkship for a judge that was not even on the bench when they clerked.

They also tend to be in high demand and might only have limited time to spend mentoring you. Moreover, you might feel constrained about how honest to be with them about the decisions you are grappling with and life challenges you are facing. After all, you may want to come to them for recommendations down the road, which is not exactly conducive to transparency in your conversations with them today.

A good rainmaker mentor is someone who believes in you and is willing to put their weight behind you. A well-known mentor who is ambivalent about you or who does not know you exist is not worth much. I know someone who worked for a high-profile lawyer before law school and she was very excited about getting him to write her a recommendation. She had left her job at this point, but she emailed asking for a recommendation. Months passed. Finally, someone from the lawyer's office called her back and explained that the lawyer did not feel like he knew her well enough to write her a recommendation. Not exactly a great mentor. You should invest in mentoring relationships where you have received signals that the other person is invested in mentoring you.

A confidant mentor fulfills a different role. They are likely to have more time to devote to you and you might feel you can talk with them about decisions that might seem too trivial to discuss with a rainmaker. But perhaps more crucially, they have a much more recent perspective on the decisions you are making, and can provide the kind of current, tailored advice that you are unlikely to get from a rainmaker. A good confidant mentor is someone willing to invest time in you and who has relevant life and career experience you can draw from. Ideally, you would have several confidant mentors so you can get a variety of perspectives.

Confidant mentors are easier to identify than rainmaker mentors. Emailing a V.I.P. out of the blue is unlikely to be effective, but many young lawyers will answer emails from people they don't know looking for advice. Identify a few people who have the job you want, or who have taken a path you want to pursue and then reach out. In addition, take advantage of any mentoring programs your law school offers. Some affinity groups also set students up with alumni or more senior students. These programs can help you connect with people who are open to mentoring.

Don't get discouraged if you don't click with a mentor right away. You have to keep at it so that one day you can be in a position to mentor others like you.

WHAT CLASSES TO TAKE

You will spend much of your time in law school studying and attending classes. After you have completed the first-year curriculum and taken a few other core courses, you will have almost complete freedom to choose what classes you want to take. This is great for public interest students who may not be particularly enthusiastic about the required courses.

The strange truth, however, is that it basically does not matter which classes you take. Law school is teaching you how to think and write like a lawyer. It is not designed to teach you what you need to know for the bar examination—you will have a separate bar review course for that. Taking "black letter" courses may be marginally beneficial for the bar, but you will need to relearn everything anyway. Most jobs you get after graduation will not require you to have taken certain courses. While many seminars will be interesting, they are rarely essential to your future practice as a lawyer. In other words, you should take the classes that interest you and not worry too much about which classes you "should" take.

There are a couple of caveats to this advice. First, you may consider taking a course with a professor who has similar interests to you and who you think might make a good mentor or recommender. Second, if there is an area of law that interests you and that you think might form part of your practice after law school, you may want to take the related law school course if it is offered. Third, you may want to take a class with a stellar professor regardless of what they teach.

Finally, there is type of course that you absolutely must take if you want to do public interest law: the law school clinic. It is likely to be one of the most influential courses you take in law school and will have a lasting effect on your career.

Law school clinics operate like small public interest organizations located within law schools and are designed to provide experiential education to law students. They are usually taught by professors, although sometimes they are taught by outside lawyers acting as adjunct instructors. They are organized around different areas of law (like housing or employment law) or around different kinds of lawyering (litigation, transactional, policy), and they take on real clients and legal matters. Most schools have limited clinical spots and you may need to apply in multiple semesters before being accepted. Some clinics only last one semester. Others allow students to stay in them until they graduate. They typically provide legal services on a pro bono basis.

There are several reasons why clinics make for superior learning experiences. The first is that clinics are structured with that goal in mind. Internships are a good way to get real legal experience, but the organization you are working for is hiring you because of what you will contribute to its work, not because of how the internship benefits you. Some public interest organizations do take an active interest in their interns, but if there is a conflict between their own priorities and the students' experience, their priorities will come first. Clinics, on the other hand, are designed to provide the maximum benefit possible for students while still complying with the clinic's ethical obligations to clients. Clinics would not exist without the students and as such, clinics prioritize the student experience.

To see how this plays out in practice, think about this example. Let's say that there is a court hearing scheduled in two weeks. It will take an experienced lawyer two hours to prepare for the hearing, while it will take a law student ten hours to prepare. In addition, if a law student does the argument, an experienced lawyer will need to spend an additional five hours preparing the student. The choice between these two options for a public interest organization is simple: the lawyer will do the argument because it will take two person-hours instead of fifteen. But a clinical professor will prepare the student to do the argument because that is what is best pedagogically for the student. The student may get something out of watching the public interest lawyer argue the case, but it will pale in comparison to the experience of actually doing the oral argument.

The second reason clinics are important is more intangible. Law school can be deeply alienating for a student who wants to take a different career path than most of their classmates. Clinics can provide an antidote to that alienation. One of your goals in law school should be to find other public interest students who can provide you with encouragement and support. Clinics attract public interest students and provide opportunities to bond with classmates because of the intensive nature of the work.

Moreover, clinics are a good way to meet and cultivate mentoring relationships with professors who can support you in your public interest career. Most clinical professors come from public interest backgrounds, and they are much more likely to have extensive experience in practice, unlike your other professors who may have only worked in practice for a year or two if at all. Clinics are usually limited to just a handful of students, and you will get to know your clinical professors much better than professors you have big lecture classes with.

The only downside of law school clinics is that they tend to be time intensive, but the work you do will be richly rewarded, both in terms of the impact you can have on real people's lives and the positive effect it will have on your own public interest career.

Another kind of experiential course that law schools sometimes offer is an externship, which is like a summer internship except it happens during the academic year and is usually accompanied by a classroom component. Externships can be a great way to spend time working at a local public interest organization. It also increases the number of organizations with whom you have a relationship when it is time to find a job. Whether making local connections is important depends on whether you plan to stay in the same geographic area after law school or whether you plan to move elsewhere.

During the pandemic, many externship programs went remote and law students were able to extern with organizations located anywhere. If remote externships remain an option after the pandemic, they could become a way for law students to work at non-local organizations during the academic year. I am skeptical, however, that a remote externship is worth your time. Part of the value of an externship is being a part of the organization, learning about the office culture, and developing social bonds, all of which are difficult to do remotely.

Externships can also fail to provide students with a high-quality experience even when they are in person. This is not always true. Some externships are excellent. But there is a much greater variety in the quality of work and supervision in externships than in clinics. Externships are supervised by practicing lawyers who are busy and focused on many things other than their interns. Clinics, on the other hand, are taught by professors whose job it is to teach law students.

A second problem with externships is that they typically require a law student to only work a few hours a week at the organization because the student also must devote time to their other classes. A few hours a week is often not enough time to truly get anything out of the externship, particularly when you account for travel time. Some schools have programs where you work full-time at an organization for a semester for academic credit, and these programs are more likely to result in a meaningful experience. For example, the State of New York runs a statewide externship program called the Pro Bono Scholars Program where third-year law students take the bar early in February and then spend March–May working full-time at a public interest organization for academic credit.[2] The more time you dedicate to an externship, the more likely you are to get something out of it.

LAW SCHOOL EXTRACURRICULAR ACTIVITIES

When you come up for air after your first semester in law school, you may start to wonder what activities you should participate in outside of classes. Yes, in law school (unlike in many graduate programs) there are a plethora of "extra-curriculars." These activities include law review, moot court, affinity groups, student government, and volunteer opportunities.

As I explained earlier, in law school, you want to focus on getting real legal experience, on proving your passion for public interest work, and on making connections that will help you get a job. You have limited time in law school, and you should not let yourself get caught up in doing something just because everyone else is. Use your time wisely to set yourself up for a public interest career. If an activity does not contribute to at least one of these three goals, it is not the best use of your time.

Law Review

For those not familiar with what law review is, here is a short primer. In most academic disciplines, academic journals are staffed and edited by academics or career professionals and articles are selected for publication through peer review. In law, academic journals (also called "law reviews") are staffed by law students, who select and edit the articles through a process that only occasionally involves peer review. A journal usually has a faculty advisor, but law students do most of the work. This work can sometimes be interesting, but much of it involves fact-

---

[2] Pro Bono Scholars Program, http://ww2.nycourts.gov/attorneys/probonoscholars/index.shtml (last accessed May 25, 2022).

checking, citation formatting and proofreading, not exactly the most thrilling tasks. Students on law review will spend long hours locating sources and verifying quotations during evening and weekend work sessions.

Law review is competitive and usually requires high grades, winning a writing competition, or both. This makes sense if you think about it. If getting on law review were not prestigious, the entire system would collapse. Getting law students to spend hours and hours doing tedious work would be a pretty hard sell if it did not come with some career benefit. Usually, the process of applying to be on law review happens in the spring of your first year of law school, but the mythmaking about the importance of law review starts the first day. By spring, you may feel compelled to apply even if six months earlier you did not even know what law review was.

For some jobs, it is an advantage to be on law review. For example, if you want to be a legal academic, you should do law review because you will learn something about the selection and publication process for legal scholarship. If you want to do a clerkship, you should do law review since many judges view it as a marker of law school success and potential. For jobs in the private sector, it is helpful (though not essential), especially for students from lower-ranked schools where it is important to distinguish yourself from your peers.

For most public interest students, the calculus is different. It is not that doing law review is bad exactly, but the advantages are fewer and the tradeoffs greater. In my experience, public interest employers do not care much about law review. Moreover, it does not advance any of the goals I outlined above. It is not real legal experience, does not prove your commitment to public interest law, and does not help you make connections in the field. What it does do is take time away from other activities that do advance those goals. You do not have unlimited time in law school and you will not be able to do every activity, at least without your grades or mental health suffering. Law review is a large time commitment and will limit what else you can do.

You may feel tempted to try out for law review anyway because it is a gold star that is hard to resist. Law students are very good at pursuing gold stars, even if it does not get them any closer to their goals. If law review is something you think you will enjoy, then by all means do it. Otherwise, there are better ways to spend your limited time in law school.

Moot Court

Moot court is a simulated oral argument and brief-writing competition that students can choose to participate in during their second and third years. You may think that moot court is essentially like getting real legal experience because you are learning how to write an appellate brief and do an oral argument. Except moot court is not real and does not really approximate actual legal work. Real lawyering is messy. It is not wrapped up for you in a tidy package. The record below is often voluminous and complicated. There sometimes is not applicable case law to draw from. If there is case law, it may be convoluted and contradictory. And then there is the small matter of actually having a client you must represent.

If you want to do appellate litigation after law school, you should absolutely do moot court because it may be difficult to get appellate experience as a law student. But most public interest lawyers do not focus on appellate practice, at least not exclusively. Perhaps more importantly, public interest employers will not view moot court as real legal experience. Unless you win the competition (and let's be honest, you probably won't), you are unlikely to see a career benefit at all.

The same goes for trial team, or trial advocacy as it is called at some schools. If you can take moot court or trial team as a course that takes the place of a lecture course or two, then do it. You will probably get more out of it that your typical law school course. But I would not do it as an extra curricular.

Student Government and Affinity Groups

Student government is another activity that law students often devote time to. It is basically like student council in high school, except that instead of ice cream socials and car washes, they plan happy hours and networking events. Let me be blunt: student government is a waste of your time. You may think that it will be a good way to make connections with faculty or alumni, and that very well may be true depending on your school. But in my experience, the connections you will make are much more likely to be in the private sector. I have never met a public interest lawyer who was very involved in student government in law school (perhaps because they had more important things to do). And while organizing raffles and planning social events may be good leadership experience in high school, it doesn't really teach you anything about being a lawyer. Go to the events they plan if you want to network; don't waste your time planning them.

Counterintuitively, the calculus is different for affinity groups, such as groups for female law students, students of color, or LGBTQ students. Public interest law disproportionately attracts women and people of color, and thus, aspiring public interest lawyers are more likely to make worthwhile connections through affinity groups than through student government. In addition, affinity groups can be places of support and mentorship for law students who might otherwise feel alienated in law school. This does not mean that you should join every single affinity group at your law school. Pick one or two and only take on a leadership role in one at most. That way you will still have plenty of time to accomplish your other law school goals.

Volunteer Work

Many law students also do volunteer work. Although it is hard to generalize, law-related volunteer experience is generally a worthwhile and strategic way to spend your extra time in law school. Not only are you getting real legal experience, but you are proving your passion by engaging in pro bono work before graduation. Non-legal volunteer work may also show commitment, especially if it is related to the area of law you eventually want to practice. For instance, teaching an art history class at a local prison isn't legal work per se, but it might help you demonstrate your commitment if you want to be a prisoners' rights lawyer. Volunteering at a domestic violence shelter could benefit a law student planning on representing domestic violence victims after law school. And, of course, volunteer work is valuable even if it doesn't give you a career advantage, something you would be hard pressed to say about moot court or student government.

You can take this too far, however. Try not to spread yourself too thin signing up for multiple volunteer activities. Choose volunteer activities consciously and with a goal in mind. That is not to say that you should not volunteer doing something completely unrelated to your career goals. Volunteer work is even more admirable when it has no immediate pay off for the person doing it. But if you find yourself juggling multiple volunteer commitments that you think will help you get a job after graduation, consider paring back to one or two.

SUMMER INTERNSHIPS

You have two summers during law school and you want to make sure to use them wisely. Applications start for first-year students in December and ramp up after the New Year. For second-year students, the application process begins much sooner, in September or October. This is a much earlier timeline that many college internships. If it is March and you do not have a summer job yet, you are behind.

How to Get a Public Interest Internship

Law schools often set up interviewing programs for students seeking private sector jobs. These programs typically are scheduled shortly before the start of fall semester. There may be a second program for first year students in January or February. Unfortunately, public interest employers rarely attend these interview programs. It could be that schools do not encourage public interest employers to participate, instead deciding to focus on the job prospects of the majority of students who will not take a public interest job. Or it could be that public interest organizations do not feel like it is necessary to attend the programs in order to attract high quality candidates. Whatever the reason, public interest students are going to have to do more work than other law students to get their summer jobs.

It is most difficult to get a public interest internship your first summer. Public interest organizations prefer students after their second year of law school because they have more skills that can be put to use. In addition, many students who ultimately go work at law firms will do a public interest internship their first summer, either because they have not yet abandoned their dreams of a public interest career or because they cannot get a summer associate position at a law firm (firms, like public interest organizations, prefer students with more experience). That means that there are more people competing for fewer positions. Your advantage will be convincing the organization that you are truly interested in their work and are not just applying because you have nothing better to do. There are also a slew of government internships that are open to students after their first year. If you think government work may be for you, your first summer is a good time to try it out.

Both government and non-profit internships are likely to be unpaid, unlike summer associate positions at law firms. This makes doing a summer internship more difficult for individuals with other personal obligations or who are not able to take out extra loans. Many law schools attempt to solve this problem by offering summer stipends for law students doing public interest internships. If your school does not advertise such a program, then you should inquire into whether there are any resources available.

If resources are not available, you should do a public interest internship even if effectively it means that you must pay for the experience. This seems very unfair and it is. The fact that students are expected to do so much unpaid work in order to get the job they want is a problem. It discourages many students from public interest careers and it makes it particularly difficult for the most disadvantaged students who may not be able to afford it. Still, you are not going to be able to solve this structural problem as a law student. You should take the unpaid internship unless you absolutely cannot.

You will want to apply to many internships in the hopes of getting one. Your second summer it will be easier to land a position, both because there are fewer people vying for them and because you (hopefully) will have a previous internship on your resume. Still, you cannot assume that you will get your top choice.

There is no centralized location to find all public interest internships. Some career development offices maintain their own lists, but they usually rely on public interest employers to inform them of internship opportunities. Many public interest organizations do not advertise their internships widely, either because they do not have to work so hard for candidates or because they are too busy doing their jobs to go out of their way. PSJD is a website that acts as a clearinghouse for public interest law opportunities (both internships and jobs),[3] but not all organizations post their internships there.

To find all internships in your preferred geographic location and/or your preferred area of law, you will likely need to do at least some research yourself. If you are lucky, organizations will post internship applications on their website, but if you do not see anything posted you should not hesitate to reach out and ask. It could be that they have not posted it. Or it could be they are not hiring interns or have already hired everyone they plan to for a given summer. As always, your mentors are a good resource for identifying potential opportunities as well.

If you are lucky enough to get multiple internship offers, you then have to decide which one to accept. There are two things you should consider when deciding which internship to accept: which internship will give you the best experience and which internship with help you most to advance your career goals. Unfortunately, these factors sometimes point in opposite directions.

First, an acknowledgement: many internships are terrible. They are poorly organized. The person running the program does not know how to manage interns or how to teach them what they need to know to do the job. Interns are given either too much responsibility or boring clerical tasks that teach them nothing. Or even worse, there is simply not enough work to do and the interns spend much of their time watching paint peel on the walls. While the organization may be great, your experience as an intern may not be.

Some internships, on the other hand, are amazing. The interns receive mentorship, guidance, and support. They are given substantive work to do and the tools they need to do it. They receive constructive feedback so that they can learn from their mistakes. They have neither too much work nor too little.

The difficulty comes in determining in advance which internships are going to be good and which are going to be bad.

---

[3] PSJD, www.psjd.org (last accessed May 20, 2022).

All organizations will say the right things to their internship candidates, but the unvarnished truth is often very different than the pitch. This is another place where mentors can be very helpful. They might have former students who either interned or worked at the organization. And they may be familiar with the broader reputation of the organization in the legal community. The career development office will also probably have a list of former students who did internships at that organization. Even if you do not know them personally, you should reach out. If your career development office does not have a list of past interns, ask the organization to connect you. You are more likely to get the truth from a former intern than from someone still at the organization.

You may also be able to glean some information about the quality of the internship program by inquiring into the organization's plans for the summer. For instance, if an organization has trainings, brown bag lunches, or other intern events on the calendar, it might indicate that it has put more thought into its program. If there is an intern coordinator who is tasked with managing the interns and their workload, that is better than if interns are assigned to individual attorneys or to no one at all.

The other factor to consider when deciding which internship to accept is to think about how each internship will advance your career goals. If there is a particular organization that you are interested in working for after graduation, doing an internship there may give you an advantage when it comes to post-graduation employment opportunities. If you are interested in pursuing work at a public defender office, an internship in criminal defense is going to be more useful than one in environmental law. There also may be some advantage in working for a bigger, better-known organization that might have more cache in the public interest community. Your mentors can help you figure out whether there is a clear advantage to choosing one internship over another.

What to Get out of an Internship

Once you accept an internship, you should then think about what you want to get out of it. First, you should think about your internal goals. Ideally, your summer experiences should help you narrow down what you want to do after you graduate. Especially if you think you know what you want to do, you should try to do that for at least one summer to see if you actually like it. Many law students come into law school with their hearts set on a particular job only to realize they actually dislike it once they try it out. If you try something and hate it, it might save you years of working at the wrong job after law school.

Another internal goal might be to gain experience or develop skills that will be helpful to you on the job market or in gaining competency in your chosen job. This is something you should think about when you are deciding where to intern as well. You should ask what skills you are likely to learn over the summer to determine whether they match up to what you want to learn how to do.

You may also have several external goals for your summer, such as developing relationships with potential recommenders or securing a sponsor for public interest fellowships after law school. Even if you do not end up working at the organization or even in same field, developing relationships is important. The public interest community is relatively small, and your summer supervisor may be the key to getting another internship or job later. You will probably get more traction from getting to know one lawyer very well as opposed to many lawyers only a little bit. If all anyone in the office can say about you is "oh, they worked on a memo for me once," then it will be hard for any one person to write a stellar recommendation.

A recommendation from a practicing public interest attorney will be very important during the fellowship and job application process. Remember, organizations cannot afford to hire dead weight. Recommendations from professors only go so far. It turns out that high achievement in the classroom does not always translate into good lawyering in the field. An organization will want to hear from someone you worked with over the summer (a clinical professor who observed you doing real legal work can also play this role).

In terms of how to impress people at your summer job, the advice probably sounds similar to the advice on how to excel at any job: be enthusiastic, be willing to go the extra mile, be a self starter, do not require constant micromanaging, be diligent and dependable. Interns do not always add value to an organization. Sometimes they take more effort to supervise than they contribute. Don't be one of those interns! Make yourself indispensable to your overworked, underpaid supervising attorneys and it will redound to your benefit.

HOW TO SURVIVE LAW SCHOOL

You went to law school because you thought a law degree would help you contribute to the world. But after the heady excitement of the first few weeks wears off, you find yourself disappointed. Your classes barely touch on anything related to your interests at all. Instead, you spend hour after hour reading old, crusty opinions written by dead judges about legal principles you could not care less about. You are surrounded by students who seem to have been born to go to law school and who always know the answers in class.

You quickly get sucked into the competition for grades, even though everything you are learning seems pointless. Suddenly, everyone is competing for summer associate jobs and even though you never wanted to work at a law firm, you start to feel nervous. Maybe you should be applying too? You alternate between feeling like you are already falling behind to thinking that maybe law school was a mistake.

The first year of law school is a rite of passage for every law student, but it can be particularly tough for public interest students. The first-year curriculum, which has not changed much in a hundred years, is not exactly designed with future public interest lawyers in mind. And because you are taking the same classes as everyone else in your law school class, the herd mentality is hard to avoid. Many public interest students end up feeling bored, anxious, alienated, and confused in their first year.

The good news is that it will get better. By your second year, you will have most of your required courses out of the way, and you will be able to pick classes that align better with your interests. You will also be able to focus less on your classes and spend more time on volunteering, experiential learning, and extra-curricular activities that will remind you why you came to law school in the first place. You will find other law students who are also hoping to chart a different path, and you will find professors and other mentors who want to support you.

Still, the first year can be tough. Here are a few suggestions to get you through it:

(1) Remember that it will get better. This may seem obvious, but not everyone understands how sui generis the first year of law school really is. It will get easier in your second year and easier still in your third year. Just knowing that your misery is temporary may help you endure it.

(2) Keep in mind that none of your classmates know what they are doing either. Avoid toxic people who will not shut up about grades, class rank, etc. Try to see it for what it is: posturing and insecurity. Feel secure in the knowledge that you know why you came to law school and nothing anyone says can change that.

(3) Don't let law school consume your life. Keep strong connections with friends and family who knew you before you went to law school and can remind you of why you went. It will be easier to resist the herd mentality if you have a social life outside of law school.

(4) Find peers in your class with similar goals. This will happen naturally in your second and third years, but you can make an effort to find other public interest students in your first year too. Although it might not seem like it, there are other students in your classes having the exact same thoughts as you. Find them as early as possible so you can commiserate together.

(5) Talk to someone who has already been through what you are experiencing. This might be a senior student or a recent graduate. Whoever it is, you want to find someone who can give you the much-needed perspective you need to stick to your goals

and not be sidetracked by what everyone else is doing.

(6) Find volunteer work that connects you to the communities you hope to serve. Some law schools discourage or prohibit first year law students from participating in extracurricular activities because they want you focusing on your classes. You definitely should not overschedule yourself during your first year of law school, but you don't need to spend every minute of every day studying. Find a way to give back that keeps you connected to your goals.

Most students who abandon their public interest dreams do so by the beginning of their second year, when students apply for law firm jobs for their second summer (many of which will turn in to permanent offers of employment). If you can remember why you came to law school during this first year, you are more likely to graduate into a job and career you actually want.

CHAPTER 5

THE JOB SEARCH

You have survived law school. Now it is time to get a job. No problem, right? This task is really two tasks in one. First, you have to figure out what you want to do. Then you have to find a job that allows you to do it. Neither of these tasks is easy.

HOW TO DECIDE WHAT KIND OF JOB YOU WANT

Many law students focus on figuring out what area of law they are interested in or what problem in the world they want to try to solve. That is important, because you want to be passionate about your work. But it is not the only question you should be asking. You also want to find a job that you enjoy doing day to day, that plays to your strengths, and that minimizes work that drains or bores you. Many jobs sound better in theory than in practice. A job you never seriously considered may end up being perfect for you. That is why you will want to spend your law school years trying out different jobs to see what works for you. Here are some questions to ask yourself when evaluating the different kinds of public interest jobs you might apply for:

What are you happiest spending your days doing? If you are a social butterfly, you will not be happy as a solo practitioner. If you are painfully shy, a job that requires you to stand up in court every day might not be a good fit. If you hate writing, being an appellate lawyer is going to be challenging. If it drains you to meet with people all day, you might not want to become a legal services attorney. It does not matter how important you think the work is if you are not happy doing it.

What are your strengths? We should always be pushing ourselves to do hard things, but you will make yourself miserable if you pick a job that does not play to your strengths. There is a lot of good work to do out there to do (more work than can possibly be done), so pick something that allows you to make a real impact.

What annoyances are manageable, and which are not? Every job has things about it that are tedious and that you would rather not do. Your job is to figure out which jobs have annoyances that you can tolerate, and which jobs have annoyances you cannot. For example, many lawyers who work for non-profit organizations have to do fundraising and very few people enjoy fundraising. Private public interest law firms will require you to bill your time, which no one enjoys. Working for the government involves all sorts of bureaucracy and red tape. Being a social entrepreneur might require you to become more well versed in accounting and tax law. Being a clinical professor has its annoyances too, like how students drop off the face of the earth when finals roll around. There is no perfect job, so you should find a job that is imperfect in the way that is right for you.

What kind of change do you want to make in the world? Not every public interest lawyer changes the world in the same way. Let's say that you are very interested in criminal justice reform. Do you want to exonerate people who were wrongly convicted? Do you want to work on sentencing reform? Do you want to pass legislation decreasing penalties for drug crimes? Each of these projects is going to lead to very different work even if the goal—"criminal justice reform"—is the same.

Another way of thinking about this question is to think about how you believe social change occurs and then find a job at an organization that operates on the same theory. To help you figure this out for yourself, read through the following statements and try to decide which statement or statements best express your view of the legal system:

1. The law is basically just.
2. The law is basically just and we have to work within the system to correct injustice when it happens.
3. The law is basically unjust and we have to work within the system to change it.
4. The law is basically unjust and we have to work outside the system to change it.

5. The law is basically unjust and we have to work to overthrow and replace the current system.

Everyone will identify with more than one of these statements in different circumstances, so the contrarian will refuse to pick a number. Rather than focusing on those different circumstances, however, you should think about the legal system impressionistically. Most of us probably have some idea about which statement most closely mirrors our general views, even if occasionally we end up agreeing with a different statement. It is important to be honest with yourself here. Some people believe they are a different number than they actually are upon reflection.

If you are still having trouble picking a statement, here is a trick that can help you figure it out. Imagine you are speaking with a client, who is unhappy with how the legal system has handled her particular legal matter. "This is just so unfair," she says. Do you find yourself wanting to say, "This is just how the system works" (1). Or do you want to say something like, "You're right, it is unfair. No legal system is perfect and it got it wrong here" (2). Or "You're right, the system is screwed up and we're trying to figure out the right case to bring in order to challenge it" (3). Or "You're right. The current system is never going to bring you justice. That's why it's so important to get together with other people in your community and force the people in power to change it" (4). Or do you say, "You're right, and nothing we do will change it. Let's go make some Molotov cocktails instead" (5). (If you think I'm kidding about the last part, you should read about the two lawyers who pled guilty to throwing Molotov cocktails into police cars during a Black Lives Matter protest.[1]) Which sounds most like something you would say?

Your number will tell you something about the kind of public interest law you will be happiest practicing. If you simply cannot choose between two numbers, then you may be happy doing more than one kind of public interest law. If you insist on picking all five numbers, go back and do the exercise again.

[1] David Thomas, New York Lawyers Plead Guilty in Molotov Cocktail Case, Reuters, Oct. 20, 2021, available at https://www.reuters.com/legal/litigation/new-york-lawyers-plead-guilty-molotov-cocktail-case-2021-10-20.

Lawyers must make lots of hard decisions, so you might as well start now. Have your number? Great.

Very few lawyers are true 5s (though some may pretend to be after a few drinks). Most revolutionaries do not go to law school. If they do, they usually quit, are tremendously unhappy, or eventually change careers. You simply cannot be a lawyer and reject the legal system entirely. Even if you could manage the cognitive dissonance, the rules of professional conduct put limits on what lawyers can ethically do.

Many lawyers are 1s. They tend to inhabit the upper echelons of the corporate world, law firms, judicial chambers, and other powerful places. In public interest lawyering, 1s are most likely drawn to work as prosecutors and government attorneys. It is much easier to believe the legal system is just if you have ended up on top. It is much easier to believe that justice is attainable when you are the one doling it out.

Other public interest lawyers cluster in the 2–4 range, but there are big differences within that range. The 2s are lawyers who do not see the injustices in the legal system as systemic. Instead, they see people with individual legal problems. The solution is often more lawyers who can bring more cases on behalf of individuals to solve these problems. 2s tend to cluster at legal services organizations, where the goal is to represent as many people as possible with limited funds, and they tend to frame their advocacy around the idea of "access to justice." In other words, they believe justice is possible in the current legal system if only people have the resources, legal or otherwise, to access it.

The 3s are the impact litigators. They see the problems in the system, but they believe that the way to change it is from within. This usually means bringing lawsuits, but it can also mean advocating for legislative reform. They tend to believe that the legal system can reform itself if confronted with persuasive enough arguments. Many private public interest law firm lawyers would also fall into this category.

The 4s are skeptical that lawyering alone can result in social change and are drawn to law and organizing work. They tend to attach themselves to social movements or grassroots organizing groups that are trying to change the system from the outside. They may also be drawn to public policy, where progress is made by changing the law not enforcing it, or to social entrepreneurship, where change occurs in the business world, not in the courtroom. 4s may wonder whether they can actually make a difference practicing law, but they still believe that the system is reformable and see both inside and outside pressure as important to attaining that goal.

It is possible to work at an organization that practices a different kind of law than your number, but a mismatch can lead to burnout or disillusionment. It can be frustrating to have a different theory of change than your organization and may lead you to feeling like you are spinning your wheels.

All of these theories of change have value. Still, believing that all public interest lawyering has value is different than deciding what kind of lawyer you will be. You need to find the place where you are most comfortable and where you will be able to do the most amount of good. You should be using your time in law school trying to figure this out—through internships, externships, law clinics, and pro bono opportunities. Hopefully, by the time you are ready to think about your career path after law school, you have some idea of where to look.

PATHWAYS INTO PUBLIC INTEREST LAW

Once you have an idea of what kind of public interest job you want, the only thing left to do is actually get a job. No problem, right? In reality, getting your first legal job will be harder than getting any other job during your career. There are a couple of reasons for this. First, you will never have less experience than you have coming out of law school, and employers generally like more experience rather than less. This is particularly true in public interest law where organizations do not have the resources to train new attorneys themselves.

Second, there are just fewer public interest jobs out there than there are people who want those jobs. This is a longstanding structural problem. Despite the fact that there is high demand for pro bono legal services, there is never enough funding to hire sufficient numbers of lawyers to meet the demand. This is a place where planning and persistence pay off.

You want to be one of the people who snags one of the few jobs there are, not one of the people who gives up or fails to do the things necessary to get a job.

There are several different strategies for getting a public interest job after law school and you may have to utilize more than one. The first strategy is to apply for public interest fellowships, which are special positions created for graduating law students or new lawyers and which fund work at an organization or government agency for a fixed period of time, usually one or two years. The second is to develop a relationship with an organization in law school—either by doing an internship, an externship, or volunteering—that then agrees to hire you after graduation. The third is to apply for open positions through job postings just as any lawyer would.

All three strategies can be successful, but it is far easier to get a job with a fellowship than it is to apply for open positions. The reason should seem familiar at this point: money. Fellowships are often outside funded, which means that organizations can essentially get a staff attorney for free. The disadvantage of fellowships is that they are usually time limited to one or two years, and there is no guarantee that your host organization will hire you after the fellowship is over.

If organizations cannot get free labor, then they at least want to hire someone who they know will be a valuable member of their team. That is where personal connections come in. If you have already proven your value, the organization will be less hesitant to take a chance on you. This is true in nearly all contexts but is particularly true in the cash-strapped non-profit world.

Applying for open positions is much more of a crapshoot, and you will need to apply to a lot of jobs to be successful. That may mean applying for jobs that are not exactly what you want to do, that pay less than you want to make, or that are not located in your preferred place to live. Just remember: your first job will not be your last (unless you want it to be). Once you have a public interest job, it will be much easier to get another one. And the difference between having no experience and 1–2 years of experience is vast. Expertise in the legal profession means something different than in other fields, in which you might need to have a decade or more of job experience before you can call yourself an "expert." I often joke that in law, an expert often means someone who has done something once, which is only a slight exaggeration. This is why taking a public interest fellowship is less of a gamble than it seems even though it may not lead to a permanent job. With 1–2 years of public interest experience under your belt, it will be much easier to get another job even if your fellowship organization cannot hire you.

There are a couple of exceptions to the general rule that it is hard to get a public interest job from an open posting straight out of the law school. Public defender offices, unlike many non-profits, are often hiring for multiple entry-level positions and do hire graduating law students in many places. If you are trying to get a job at a start-up or a new non-profit organization, they may be more willing to take a chance on a lawyer without much experience. Legislative staffers are hired directly out of law school, both at the state and federal level.

There are also some jobs that are very hard to get straight out of law school. For example, it is very hard to get a job as an attorney at a U.S. Attorney's Office without some legal experience. Established companies with a social justice mission are unlikely to hire someone as in-house counsel right out of law school. It is nigh impossible to get a job as a clinical professor without at least five years practice experience.

There are, of course, exceptions to these general rules. Personal connections can turn even the most unattainable job offer into a reality. But before you get your heart set on a particular job, you should make sure it is an realistic goal. If it is not, hope is not lost. You just need to identify a good steppingstone to your ultimate goal and then work towards that. Do not just assume you know what a good steppingstone is! Ask people currently doing your dream job how they and others they know got there. There is no reason to reinvent the wheel if you do not have to.

The timeline for these different strategies means that while you may need to use more than one of them, you will not have to be doing it all at once. Fellowship applications are due in the summer or fall before you graduate. You can have conversations with organizations you have relationships with throughout your third year of law school. Open postings generally want candidates to be able to start immediately, which means you cannot realistically begin applying for them until you are close to graduation or while you are studying for the bar.

There are several common mistakes that law students make in the job search. The first is not to apply for fellowships. Some students are simply not thinking about their job search until the middle of their third year after the deadlines for most fellowships have passed. Or they do not think that they are competitive for fellowships and so decide not to apply. The first problem is easy to fix—read this book at the beginning of law school so that you know to start thinking about fellowships in the spring of your second year.

Solving the second problem takes a shift in perspective. Yes, it is true that many fellowships are competitive, but many are no more competitive than the open positions you will have to apply for later. Some open positions might be more competitive because you will be competing against more experienced attorneys rather than other graduating law students.

There is also value in applying for fellowships even if your odds of getting one are low. The application process will allow you to make connections with organizations who potentially could end up hiring you anyway. I know plenty of people who ended up getting offered a staff attorney position after going through the fellowship process with an organization and several other people who ended up working for that organization a few years down the line. You can never underestimate how important it is to make personal connections. Once an organization has gone through the fellowship process, they will feel invested in you. Sometimes an organization will not be able to cobble the money together to hire you, but sometimes they will. It is worth a shot.

Another mistake law students make is that they give up the job search too early and take a private sector job they do not want, which diverts them from their goal of practicing public interest law. Many law students will have offers in hand from the law firm they worked for their second summer when they return to campus in the fall. That puts enormous pressure on public interest students to find a job, any job, as winter transitions into spring. Add in the looming threat of student loan payments and many students buckle under the pressure.

I am not going to suggest that you do not need to worry about getting a job. But I will suggest that you have longer than you think to get a job lined up. After graduation, you will spend 2–3 months studying for the bar, during which time you cannot start a new job. Your student loans are in deferment until six months after graduation. You do not need to take a job you do not want in February before you graduate. If it gets to June or July and you still have no leads, you may need to compromise. If possible, you should compromise by taking a public interest job even if it is not exactly what you want to do. It will be easier to transition to another public interest job later.

If you absolutely must take a private sector job, you should continue to apply for public interest jobs. And if you get offered a job after you have accepted another job but before you start, you absolutely can back out and take the job you want. If you have already started, even if it's only been a few months, you can transition into the job you want. There is no rule that you need to spend one or two years doing a job you do not like.

Many people find this advice distasteful and feel that they owe something to their current or future employer that precludes them from putting their own career aspirations first. Many times, they have heard this from managers at past jobs, who have an interest in getting good employees to stay. Trust me, they will be able to find someone else to replace you. You are less essential than you think. You work for an institution, not an individual and your manager would leave in a heartbeat if they got a better job. Likewise, if you get an offer for a job you like better two or three months into a new job, take it.

PUBLIC INTEREST FELLOWSHIPS

There are several different kinds of public interest fellowships and the process for applying varies depending on which kind of fellowship you are talking about.

Many of the biggest fellowship programs are separate foundations that fund recent law graduates to work at other public interest organizations. Some of the most well known of these fellowships are the Skadden Fellowship,[2] the Equal Justice Works Fellowship,[3] and the Justice Catalyst Fellowship.[4] These national fellowships tend to be very competitive, but there are sometimes local fellowships (funded through the local bar association, for example) that are easier to get. There are also some fellowships that are focused on a particular area of law. The Immigrant Justice Corps is a fellowship program founded by the late-Judge Robert Katzman to fund fellowships for recent law graduates in immigration law.[5] The Soros Justice Advocacy Fellowships fund criminal justice reform projects.[6]

Before you get very far into the process, you should check to make sure the fellowship programs you are applying for fund the kind of work you want to do. Many programs, for example, will not fund criminal defense work and they may have other limitations as well. You should also be aware that most fellowships require an applicant to either be graduating from law school or, at most, have one year of experience. Usually, judicial clerkships do not count, but other jobs will. Thus, if you go work at a law firm, even if it is just for a couple of years, you will likely be ineligible for most public interest fellowships, which will make it harder for you to break into the public interest world.

These outside-funded fellowship programs usually require that you identify a sponsor organization before you can apply to the fellowships. Because sponsor organizations are limited in the number of people they can sponsor (usually one per fellowship), there is often a separate application process before the fellowship application process where organizations choose which candidates to sponsor. Not all organizations are this deliberate. Some organizations will realize late that they need to find a

---

[2] Skadden Fellowship Foundation, https://www.skaddenfellowships.org (last accessed May 20, 2022).

[3] Equal Justice Works, https://www.equaljusticeworks.org/become-a-fellow (last accessed May 20, 2022).

[4] Justice Catalyst Fellowship, https://justicecatalyst.org/fellowship/jc-fellowship (last accessed May 20, 2022).

[5] Immigrant Justice Corps, https://justicecorps.org/justice-fellowship (last accessed May 20, 2022).

[6] Soros Justice Fellowships, https://www.opensocietyfoundations.org/grants/soros-justice-fellowships (last accessed May 20, 2022).

candidate to sponsor and they will scramble to find someone. Some organizations have no process at all and only sponsor a fellow when someone reaches out. If none of your early prospects pan out, you can always contact more organizations later. But starting the process early will give you more options and will allow you greater control over the process.

A good place to start is to ask about fellowship opportunities at the organization where you are interning after your second year of law school (hopefully you have taken my advice and are working in public interest rather than at a law firm). You should arrange to meet with your internship coordinator early in the summer and ask for advice about what organizations to apply to. You can also ask about their process for sponsoring fellows. They may not have worked with you long enough to have decided whether they want to sponsor you, but it will put you on their radar as they start their selection process.

Unless you have a commitment from an organization that they will sponsor you, you will need to apply to multiple organizations. Just because you volunteered or interned at an organization does not mean it will sponsor you for a fellowship. The organization has many interns and volunteers but will probably only be able to sponsor one or two people for fellowships. The way you develop a list of organizations to apply to is similar to how you develop a list of which summer internships to apply to: do your research, ask mentors and peers, and look on PSJD.[7] The organization you are interning with is also a good resource if they are working in the area that you would like to end up in. They will know what other organizations are doing good work, both locally and sometimes nationally as well.

Many outside-funded fellowships require applicants to put together a project proposal explaining what they plan to do during their fellowship. These fellowship programs do not want to fund you to become a regular staff attorney at the organization. Rather, they want you to expand the organization's work in some way. The project proposal is a joint endeavor by the sponsor organization and the applicant. The

---

7 PSJD, www.psjd.org (last accessed May 20, 2022).

fellowship program is funding the project and the organization just as much as the applicant.

Sometimes a sponsor organization's application process includes some discussion of what your proposed project will be. They may ask you to provide project ideas in advance or at the interview. This discussion is a little like a dance. The organization might have priorities in mind for what they want a fellow to work on or they may be open to what the candidate wants to work on. When talking to an organization about a potential sponsorship, you should ask whether they have identified priorities or not. Unfortunately, an organization may not tell you what their priorities are because they are looking for a candidate who is genuinely excited about the project, not just someone who pretends to be in order to get sponsored.

Other organizations do not particularly care about what project you propose as long as you can get funded. These organizations may see the requirement that fellows come up with a project as a tedious but necessary part of getting a fellow. They might prefer an additional staff attorney who can contribute to all of the organization's work, not to just a single project that has enthused funders. They may have no intention of actually having the fellow work on their proposed project. Indeed, few fellowship programs will confirm that a project actually gets completed after the fellowship is awarded. Again, you will need to try to figure out whether an organization you are applying to cares about the project proposal or not. If they do not, it would benefit you not to focus too much on possible projects.

For the most part, it helps to not be too focused in terms of what you want to do so that organizations with different priorities will be able to see how you fit into their plan. You will have to have some idea about what kind of work you want to do after graduation to even identify potential sponsor organizations. If you find yourself unsure or divided between two different areas of law or kinds of lawyering, now is the time to figure it out. But in terms of the particulars of what your project will be—e.g., in the example of housing law, whether you will focus on mold issues or inadequate heating in public housing—it is best to stay open. If the project that your organization wants you to work on is in the ballpark of what you are interested in, you will be able to make it your own.

In other words, when approaching potential sponsor organizations, you want to seem flexible, but not apathetic, interested in many projects, but not too committed to any particular one. If this sounds headache inducing, well, it is. But it is a necessary step in the process. You need a letter from a sponsor organization to continue with the process.

This advice assumes that your primary goal is locking down a sponsor organization. If you have strong opinions about what your project is and whether you will be allowed to work on it, then you should absolutely express those opinions in the application process. This is a high-risk, high-reward strategy, however, because if you are too picky you might end up without a sponsor organization at all.

Another question that you might want to ask during the fellowship process is whether they ever hire their fellows full time after their fellowships. Organizations are not required to do this and they often don't. But some organizations make it a policy to try to keep fellows on if they have done good work and the budget allows it. If you are deciding between two organizations, it might help you make the decision. While you will be able to get another public interest job after your fellowship, it will be easier if you do not have to.

Once you find a sponsor organization, you then have to write your application, including a project proposal if it is a project-based fellowship. Because these fellowships have application deadlines in September and October, you have to start working on your project proposal in July or August, especially because the project proposal will be a collaborative effort between you and your host organization. That means you need to nail down a host organization in June or July. The host organization might have its own internal deadlines for determining whom they will sponsor, and you may need to apply to several different organizations in the hopes that one of them decides to sponsor you. That means that you really should start identifying potential sponsors and reaching out to them to find out about their process in May, fifteen months before you would begin a fellowship.

If the outside-funded fellowships do not pan out, you will need to pivot to other fellowship opportunities. Some schools have fellowships for students who were not able to secure outside funding,[8] and most of these fellowships get awarded in the spring after the other fellowship processes conclude. Many require you to have applied for other fellowships first, which is another reason to apply to the national fellowships even if you do not think you have a high chance of getting one. Your sponsor organization for the outside-funded fellowships may also sponsor you for the school fellowships. Sometimes, you will end up going with a different sponsoring organization. School fellowships may also be useful for law students who want to work in an area that the national fellowships do not fund.

Some public interest organizations have their own internally-funded fellowships and they usually post these in the fall before a September start date. Organizations use these fellowship programs as a way to make entry-level hires. They know that many students will be applying for other fellowships and may not want to wait until the summer to apply for open positions. The organization fellowship model was created so that organizations could compete with the national fellowships for the public interest students. Organizations also like the flexibility of a one- or two-year probationary period that allows them to decide whether to keep the fellow on permanently. If you become a crucial part of the organization's work, chances are funding will materialize for you to stay on after your fellowship is over. If you turn out to be a problem, it provides the organization with an easy way to force you to move on.

If you know what organization you want to work for and it has a fellowship, you should apply. The advantage of these fellowships is that you do not have to do the two-step process of finding a host organization and a fellowship funder. The host organization is the funder. Many of these fellowships are not project based, which makes sense given that it is outside funders, not organizations, that have created the project-based

---

[8] For an incomplete list of the law schools with post-graduate fellowships, see American Bar Association, Post-Graduate Fellowships & Awards, https://www.americanbar.org/groups/center-pro-bono/resources/directory_of_law_school_public_interest_pro_bono_programs/definitions/pi_postgrad_fellowships (last accessed May 20, 2022).

fellowship model. Moreover, you will not be competing with more experienced attorneys as you would be with open postings. The disadvantage is that unlike staff attorney positions, these fellowships are usually limited to one or two years, after which you need to go through another hiring process or move to a different job.

If you are interested in starting your own organization as a social entrepreneur, another option worth considering is echoing green, which funds law graduates to start projects not connected to existing organizations.[9] While this is probably not an option for most law students, it can be the perfect opportunity for the right person.

Government agencies also have fellowship programs that you can apply for. One of the most well known of these programs is the U.S. Department of Justice Honors Program,[10] which is how DOJ hires most of its entry-level attorneys. Unlike non-profit programs, the Honors Program leads to a permanent position after the fellowship is over. The application deadlines for government fellowships vary, but the federal program has an early fall deadline similar to the national public interest fellowships. Local and state governments may also have fellowship programs as do some other federal agencies.[11]

The Fellowship Project Proposal

The centerpiece of an application for a project-based fellowship is the project proposal. Not all fellowships are project-based, but it's important to understand what makes a good proposal for those that are.

Every fellowship has different requirements for what needs to go into a project proposal, but at a minimum every proposal must identify: (1) the client population to be served; (2) the area of law; and (3) the types of legal services provided.

---

9 Echoing green, https://echoinggreen.org/fellowship (last accessed May 20, 2022).

10 Department of Justice, Attorney General Honors Program, https://www.justice.gov/legal-careers/entry-level-attorneys (last accessed May 20, 2022).

11 *See, e.g.*, Department of Labor Honors Program, https://www.dol.gov/agencies/sol/careers/honors-program (last accessed May 20, 2022).

For example, in recent years, the Skadden Fellowship has funded fellows who will:

- "enforce the rights of LGBTQ foster youth in dependency proceedings in Los Angeles to secure gender-affirming care for transgender and gender non-conforming youth and appropriate foster placements for all LGBTQ youth."
- "represent low-income St. Louis homeowners burdened with unfair property tax burdens. Direct assistance will include challenging assessments, foreclosure defense, and claiming excess funds from forced sales."
- "provide direct, coordinated, and bilingual debt collection defense and bankruptcy assistance for low-income DC residents hardest hit by the COVID-19 pandemic."

For each of these projects, you immediately know who the fellow will represent, what legal issues they will address, and what they will be doing.

You may be thinking, "But why do I need to come up with a project at all? I know what organization I want to work for, but I don't know yet what work I want to do. And I want to get lots of different experiences my first few years out of law school, not devote all my time to a single project."

Here is my best defense of the idea of a project-based fellowship. First, the process of drafting a project proposal prepares you for the work you are going to do. You will need to understand the problem, learn the law, and make connections in the field. If you meet your project goals, you will develop expertise and you may even become the go-to person in your area for that kind of legal work. It gives your work a kind of structure that you don't get if you just become a staff attorney. And as long as your organization allows it, your project will not preclude you from exploring the other work that the organization is doing.

Regardless of whether you come into the fellowship process excited about creating a project, you should muster up some enthusiasm. Fellowship committees will be able to tell if an applicant is ambivalent about the project they are proposing. You have to play the game in order to get the coveted prize at the end of the process: a public interest job.

The Three-Legged Stool

Once you figure out this basis information, you'll need to develop your project proposal around the idea of a three-legged stool, which requires that you convincingly answer the following three questions:

(1) Why is this work important? You will need to convince the fellowship committee that you will be fulfilling a real need that they feel compelled to fund. For better or worse, committees are often drawn to high-profile or novel problems. If you want to work on a long-standing problem (homelessness, for example), you will need to find a way to make it seem fresh. When they read about the problem you will address, the first thing they should think is "Something must be done." That something is funding you.

Sometimes, you will need to convince fellowship committees that you have identified a real problem, but more often you will need to convince them that your proposed project is a solution. You should be able to answer the question: "How will this project address this issue?" If you can't, you will need to do some more thinking.

(2) Why should I be the one doing this work? Fellowship committees might get multiple applications proposing similar projects, so you need to convince them that you are uniquely qualified to do the work. That might mean highlighting your skills, background, experience, or a combination of all three. It also means convincing the committee that you are capable of accomplishing what you set out to do. They may use your grade point average or your school as a heuristic to make that determination, but you should make the case in your application as well.

There has been a trend toward funding projects where the work connects to the personal story of the applicant, for example, a formerly incarcerated person who seeks to work to improve prison conditions, or a person whose mother worked as a domestic worker who proposes tackling wage theft in the domestic services industry. Overall, this is a good development because it centers people affected by injustice in the fight against it and diversifies the public interest world.

However, you should not feel like you cannot propose a project unless you have a personal connection to it. We are not limited to addressing problems that we ourselves have suffered. If you find yourself in this position, though, you will want to make sure to get feedback from people who are from affected populations to ensure your project is feasible, that it responds to a real need, and that you have not inadvertently missed crucial information or context. You should develop a project with, not for, the people closest to the problem.

Do not attempt to manufacture a personal connection if you do not have one. No one is going to be convinced that you should do a project working with low-income immigrants because you have a relative who came over on the Mayflower. If you do not have personal experience, you will need to think of another way to convince funders that you are the right person for the project. This is where summer internships and experience in law school clinics come in. You should explain why you became interested in the topic, even if you cannot tell a story about how the issue has affected you personally.

If you do have personal experience with a topic, do not feel shy about using it to convince funders that you are the right person for the fellowship. Learning how to tell your story in a compelling way and how it connects to the work is an important skill for you to learn to have success on the public interest job market. You do not have to share every detail but try to get comfortable telling a version of it.

If you have neither personal nor relevant legal experience, it will be very difficult to convince funders that you are the person who they should fund to do the work. You should probably go back to the drawing board and come up with a project that allows you to tell a compelling story.

(3) Why is my organization the right place to do the work? The fellowship committee must be convinced that your organization is an appropriate sponsor for your project.

Fellowship committees are looking for organizations that will provide fellows with sufficient supervision and support. You should start by looking at whether your organization has successfully sponsored fellows in the past. If it has, you will know that your organization has already developed a track record as a sponsor. If you find out that your organization has not had fellows in the past, you may need to do some work to convince the fellowship committee to take a chance on an unproven organization. You may want to have your recommenders discuss the organization in their letters for you if they are familiar with the organization. Or you may want to get someone from a different organization that has had fellows to vouch for your organization. Identifying a person who can do this is hard, but your organization should be able to help. Remember, they have skin in the game too. They want you to get the fellowship!

If you are working with a sponsor organization that has not gone through the process before, you may need to explain what they need to do and say to be found worthy. Because you have no way of knowing this yourself as someone going through the process for the first time, you should ask your mentors or recommenders for advice and then pass it on to the organization. You should make it as easy as possible for them to do what they need to do.

It is also important to make sure that your project proposal is a good fit for the organization. Do not propose doing a police reform project at an elder law non-profit, for example. It has to be related enough to the organization's current work that there will be someone at the organization who is able to supervise you. If there is a mismatch between the organization's current work and the proposed project, the organization will need to convince funders that it is an appropriate sponsor in the organization's letter.

Much of whether an organization is a good fit for a project, however, is out of your control. For example, you cannot control what fellowship committees think about your organization. Maybe a past fellow gave the organization poor reviews and they are wary of funding another fellow. You probably will never even find out that this is a reason that you were not selected. Still, you should try to anticipate concerns that the funders will have and try to respond to them in your proposal.

Once you figure out how to answer the three questions, you will need to write your proposal. Because every fellowship has very different requirements, you may end up writing multiple versions of the same project proposal. Given the different project formats, this book cannot tell you what a good proposal looks like and what it will include. To figure this out for yourself, you should always try to get your hands on another project proposal written by a successful fellowship applicant. Sometimes career development offices will have them. If it they do not, you should contact former fellows (with a connection to you, your school, or your host organization if possible) and ask if they will send theirs to you. They may say no, but it is worth asking anyway. It will be invaluable to you as you write yours.

Do not assume that you can dash off a fellowship proposal in a few days or a week. The best project proposals are thoroughly researched and have been vetted by former fellows, your organization, other people working in the field, and your mentors. You should plan to spend a month, if not more, perfecting your application.

The Fellowship Interview

The interview for project-based fellowships is similar to other job interviews in some ways. You want to seem likeable, smart, and dedicated, just like you would for any job. One difference between regular job interviews and fellowship interviews is that the committee will expect you to be an expert on your project and any related area of law. You should be prepared not only to answer any questions about the project itself, but also be able to handle broader policy or strategy questions and be familiar with any recent news or court decisions on the topic.

This may seem unfair. After all, you are not an expert. You are just graduating from law school! From the committee's perspective, however, they have many candidates applying for the same fellowship and they want to know that you will be able to make good on the promises in your project proposal. If you seem confused, unsure, or unknowledgeable, they will take it as a sign that you will be that way after starting the fellowship as well.

This means that you do not just need to brush up on the details of your resume before the interview, but also you should study for the interview like you would an exam where the subject material is your project proposal. You may not get a super hard policy question in the interview or be asked to comment on the latest Supreme Court decision related to your topic, but if you are, you want to be prepared.

The interview is also a good time to provide more information about your project than you were able to provide in the written proposal. Some fellowships have strict word limits for their applications, which means there may be some details you could not include. Even if you did not have a strict word limit, it can be good to have a few extra things to say that were not in the proposal so you do not feel like you are repeating yourself in the interview.

JUDICIAL CLERKSHIPS

Judicial law clerks work for a judge for a year or two after graduating from law school. They write memos for the judge, draft opinions and orders, and provide logistical support for the judge's courtroom. Most judges—state, federal, magistrate, and administrative—have law clerks, though not all of them have clerks they hire for a year at a time (term clerks). Some hire law clerks who hold their positions indefinitely (called career or permanent clerks). This book focuses on term clerkships because this is generally what people are talking about when they talk about clerkships in law school. Doing a clerkship after law school has become more common over time. According to the American Bar Association, 9.5% of graduating law students did a judicial clerkship after graduation in 2021.[12] Other law graduates will do a clerkship after practicing for several years.

Judicial clerkships are coveted positions that signal prestige, accomplishment, and potential. Lawyers who clerk will earn hefty bonuses if they go on to work at a big law firm. Clerkships are also important for those wanting to become law

[12] American Bar Association, Profile of the Legal Profession 58 (2021).

professors (over half of law professors hired in 2022 did at least one clerkship).[13] If you want to be an appellate lawyer or have an active Supreme Court practice, having a clerkship on your resume is crucial.

But that is generally not the case for other kinds of public interest lawyers. There may be a few circumstances where it will be an advantage. There are fellowships (such as the Skadden Fellowship) and national organizations (such as the ACLU) where having done a clerkship is an advantage. The same goes for some government jobs, particularly prestigious jobs like the U.S. Department of Justice Honors Program. But even there, it is not necessary. Most organizations are going to be much more interested in your previous public interest experience, your lawyering skills, your grades, and your passion for the work.

So is there any reason not to do a clerkship if the opportunity arises? Probably not. Getting a clerkship is difficult and most people will not get one, but there is very little downside to doing one if the option is available to you.

I did two clerkships, one with a federal district judge and one with a federal appellate judge. Clerking did not come naturally to me. It required me to pretend that law can be neutral and objective, which I do not believe. I had to feign a judicial temperament, which I definitely do not have (as anyone who knows me can attest). At times, I had to write things I did not believe, which was excruciating. But I learned so much that I would do it again in a heartbeat. I became a much better writer and legal thinker over the course of two years. Although I had taken courses in criminal and civil procedure in law school, I had absolutely no sense for how it worked in practice until I spent a year inside a courtroom. It taught me to think like a judge, which while painful at the time, has come in handy many times since. I learned how to distinguish good lawyering from bad lawyering (and there was a lot of bad lawyering). The experience was invaluable. It also would have been completely fine if I had not done a clerkship.

---

[13] Entry Level Hiring Report, https://prawfsblawg.blogs.com/prawfsblawg/entry-level-hiring-report (last accessed on May 25, 2022).

If you are thinking about applying, here are some things to keep in mind. First, there are only so many federal appellate clerkships, so you should think broadly about which clerkships to apply to. Magistrate judges, state court judges, and administrative law judges can all provide excellent clerkship experiences.

Moreover, you should consider what your plans are after clerking when deciding where to apply. If you want to be a public defender, a clerkship with a trial court is going to be much more useful than an appellate clerkship. If you want to practice in a particular area of administrative law, clerking for an administrative law judge in that area will be more helpful than other clerkships.

You should also expand the geographic scope of your search if your personal circumstances allow for it. You can live anywhere for a year. Trust me.

Finally, you should not assume that if you do not get a clerkship the year after you graduate from law school, you will never get one. I know plenty of people that clerked two, three, or four years out of law school. Judges appreciate law clerks with a little more experience. Especially if you do a two-year public interest fellowship that doesn't lead to a permanent job, a clerkship can give you time to figure out your next move.

And if it does not work out? Don't sweat it. There are many important things you will want to do if you're an aspiring public interest lawyer and clerking is pretty far down the list. It is a nice-to-have, not a must-have, on your resume.

CHAPTER 6

AFTER LAW SCHOOL

Hopefully, you have been able to snag a public interest job by the time you graduate from law school and your journey to a rewarding public interest career is well underway. Even if you do not yet have the job of your dreams, you are one step closer to getting it. Remember, your first job is the hardest to get. In just a few years' time, you will transition from a new attorney to an experienced attorney and a world of opportunities will open up to you.

That does not mean that there will not be speed bumps along the way. This section discusses several issues that may come up in the early years of a public interest lawyer's career.

LIVING ON A PUBLIC INTEREST SALARY

One of the most omnipresent and pressing concerns of young public interest lawyers is how to live a good life on a public interest salary. The misconception that you cannot is one reason so many law students abandon their public interest dreams in law school. The truth is you can live very well on a public interest salary. You just need to be careful about what your expectations are and who you are comparing your lifestyle to.

First, let's take a look at the numbers. Entry-level public interest law jobs pay an average of $48,000 for civil legal services jobs, $50,000 at other public interest organizations, $56,000 for prosecutors, and $58,000 for public defenders.[1] Compare that to the median salary of $35,000 in the United States overall.[2] If more than half of the country can live on less than your entry-level salary, you can too.

When people say they cannot afford to live on this salary, one of two things is usually going on. First, there may be some individual circumstances that make it more difficult than average. If you are supporting a large family, are a single parent,

---

1 American Bar Association, Profile of the Legal Profession 50 (2021).

2 Federal Reserve Economic Data, https://fred.stlouisfed.org/series/MEPAINUSA672N (last accessed May 24, 2022).

or have expensive health problems, your financial needs will be greater. Geographic area also matters a lot. Money stretches a lot farther in places other than San Francisco and New York, though salaries are higher in those areas as well. For example, in the Northeast, entry legal services jobs pay an average of $58,000 or $10,000 more than the national average.[3]

But most of the time, when people say they cannot afford to live on a public interest salary, they are comparing public interest and law firm salaries and are making a calculus about how important money is to them. It is not that they cannot afford to live on a public interest salary. It is just that they do not want to.

It is true that if you go into public interest law, you will make less than your classmates who go work at law firms, but how much less depends mightily on what your options are. The largest law firms (defined by the ABA as over 700 lawyers) pay first-year associates an average of $190,000 per year. However, law firms of less than 50 lawyers pay much less, an average of $85,000 per year.[4] While a lot of ink is spilled on "Big Law," most lawyers work for smaller firms. The magnitude of the difference in salaries really depends on what kind of law firm you are comparing public interest salaries to.

Still, there is a difference in salaries. If your goal is to maximize your salary, then public interest law is not for you. The reason to pursue a public interest career despite the lower salary is because you value other aspects of the job more, such as the ability to do meaningful work, to contribute to the public good, or to work on legal issues that are important to you.

Those benefits may seem like cold comfort if you are living in poverty, but public interest lawyers only live in "poverty" if you have very high expectations for your standard of living. If you feel like you must rent an expensive loft apartment in the hippest neighborhood in the city, eschew public transit for nice cars and expensive taxi rides, stay at five-resorts on your monthly international vacations, wear luxury clothes and jewelry, and spend thousands on fine wines or other expensive

---

[3] American Bar Association, Profile of the Legal Profession 49 (2021).

[4] *Id.* at 48.

hobbies, then a public interest salary will seem insufficient. You will be hard pressed to afford all of these things on a public interest salary. But you will be able to live a good, if slightly more modest, life.

The ultimate proof that it is possible to live a good life as a public interest attorney is that thousands of lawyers are already doing it. And it is not only lawyers without debt. Many public interest lawyers do have debt and they make it work. If you think you cannot, then you might want to interrogate your own expectations.

Many people may agree that they can live on a public interest salary when they are young and unencumbered but worry that they will not be able to support a family. I do not want to diminish this concern, which is particularly acute for people who go to law school later in life after they have had a family. But an entry level salary is the least you will ever make. Your salary will go up over time. It will grow with your growing financial obligations as you transition from early to mid-career.

For example, legal aid lawyers with 11 to 15 years of experience make an average of nearly $70,000.[5] It is not uncommon for senior attorneys at public interest organizations to make six-figure salaries. A spreadsheet privately circulated in the public interest legal community to help with salary transparency noted salaries up to $147,000 for senior public interest lawyers. You probably will not buy a yacht with that salary, but it is more than enough to raise a family on, including paying for piano lessons and taking family vacations.

That is not to say money should be irrelevant to your career choices. If salary is important to you, there are ways to maximize your salary within the public interest world. One common way is to take on a leadership role at your non-profit organization. Some organizations pay more than others and you can make it your goal to get a job at one of the higher paying ones. You can and should negotiate for a higher salary at your current organization. You may decide to transition out of a lower-paying public interest job such as legal services into a higher paying one doing impact litigation. You could decide to spend a few years

[5] *Id.* at 50.

making more at a private public interest law firm. You could do a short stint in government. You may decide to take on outside work, like consulting or teaching.

On the other side of the ledger, there are ways to minimize your expenses so you can live better with less. Each person's circumstances are different, so you will need to find strategies that work for you, but some ideas include living in smaller cities outside of major metropolitan areas, living in more affordable neighborhoods, sending your kids to public school, buying a less expensive home, and not eating out every night. Perhaps most importantly, you must graduate from law school with a plan for how you are going to pay your student loans that does not require you to compromise your career aspirations. If you are still unsure if you can make it work, ask an older public interest lawyer. They will be able to tell you how it has worked for them.

You may decide that you are unwilling to make the financial trade-offs necessary to have a public interest career. If so, it is important to know that about yourself. But you should not fool yourself about the choice you are making. If you are someone who would go into public interest law but for the salary, you are choosing material wealth over your other values. This, at the end of the day, is why public interest jobs are so much harder to get than other law jobs even though they pay less. People are willing to sacrifice a great deal of money to have a career that that they feel is meaningful and important. The question you must ask yourself is: are you?

With careful planning, you can enjoy a high quality of life as a public interest attorney and reap the intangible rewards that come with finding meaning and purpose in your professional life.

WORK-LIFE BALANCE

Another common concern that aspiring public interest attorneys often have is whether they will be able to balance their careers with the other parts of their life, such as family, social life, and personal pursuits.

First, the good news: it is much easier to have good work-life balance in public interest law than it is in many private sector jobs. The billable hour is the enemy of work-life balance. In most public interest jobs, you only have to track your time if you are bringing fee-generating cases. The sheer number of hours you have to work to meet the hours requirements at most law firms makes it very difficult to achieve work-life balance. Public interest lawyers work fewer hours than corporate lawyers and, hence, they have more time in their lives for other things.

Moreover, the billable hour is an extremely inflexible measure of productivity. An hour is an hour, no matter how you spend it. It may take an experienced attorney an hour to do what would take a first-year associate four or five hours. But that does not mean that you can work less. You just have three to four extra hours to take on additional work. In public interest law, if you are more productive, you can work fewer hours.

Still, that does not mean that public interest lawyers do not struggle with work-life balance. Being a lawyer means you are never truly off the clock. If a client emergency happens in the middle of the night or on your honeymoon, you are duty-bound to handle it. When you are a public interest lawyer, your clients are perhaps more likely to have emergencies given the precariousness of their lives. This can be disruptive to the other parts of your life.

And while public interest lawyers *can* work less than other lawyers, they may feel compelled to work more because they care deeply about the work. It is very hard to say no to a prospective client who is at risk of deportation, eviction, or incarceration because you are trying to carve out time for hobbies or want to preserve your weekends. Overextending yourself may make work-life balance hard to achieve and may lead to burnout, which I discuss in the next section.

Even if your hours are reasonable, your work may still take a toll on your family life. In her recent book, *Ambitious Like a Mother*, Lara Bazelon, a clinical professor who works to free innocent people wrongly convicted of crimes, talks about this struggle and the effect her commitment to her work has had on her marriage and her kids. During a particularly intense case to get a wrongful conviction overturned, she writes that:

> there was a limit to my ability to hold my outrage, fear, and stress in check. An innocent client is a fire in the brain. It crackles and consumes. Sometimes when I was

> with my children or my husband, I was unable to track what they were saying or pay close attention to what they were doing. It was difficult for me to focus on anyone or anything else, including the three of them—the most important people in my life.[6]

You can learn how to have a good work-life balance despite these challenges. The most important thing you can do is simply decide the work-life balance is important to you and then enforce your boundaries religiously. This is a skill and it takes practice. You can begin to learn how to do it in law school, and you will probably need to relearn it in each new environment in which you work.

It is also important to find a job that gives you the flexibility. As Laura Vanderkam found in the research for her book, *I Know How She Does It: How Successful Women Make the Most of Their Time*, for many professionals, it is not the number of hours worked but rather lack of flexibility that leads to poor work-life balance (unsurprisingly, she found lawyers subject to billable hours requirements to have more trouble than most working professionals with keeping work responsibilities manageable).[7]

The pandemic was, among other things, a grand experiment in alternative working arrangements. Many organizations plan to make these changed expectations permanent. Find an organization that allows you to work remotely some days, or that allows you to leave early to attend the occasional soccer game or school play, or that allows you to work a few hours on the weekend in exchange for an afternoon off or to flex your hours week to week so that a busy week can be followed by a light one. There will be some fixed commitments—court dates, filing deadlines, client meetings—but most public interest jobs allow for a high degree of flexibility in when and where the work gets done. Public interest organizations tend to put a greater value on having happy employees than other employers, in part because they know their employees could be making more money elsewhere.

---

[6] LARA BAZELON, AMBITIOUS LIKE A MOTHER: WHY PRIORITIZING YOUR CAREER IS GOOD FOR YOUR KIDS 115 (2022).

[7] LARA VANDERKAM, I KNOW HOW SHE DOES IT: HOW SUCCESSFUL WOMEN MAKE THE MOST OF THEIR TIME (2015).

Your ability to control your own work will also grow over the course of your career. As a new attorney, you may be at the whim of a supervisor who does not respect your boundaries. When last minute work occurs, you may get stuck with it because you are the most junior person. It can be hard to say no to your boss. This changes as you gain more experience and rise in the organizational hierarchy. You may become the supervising attorney. Even if you do not, your supervisor is likely to trust you more and subject you to less micromanaging. You may even have people who work for you that can step in to help. Just remember that they also want to have good work-life balance.

It is important to understand what is achievable and what is not. Work-life balance does not mean that every aspect of your life is perfectly balanced at all times. It does mean that it balances out over time. There will be months where you are working long hours and are not spending as much time with your family as you would like. These periods are almost unavoidable for lawyers. In a balanced life, however, there will also be periods where you can focus more on other parts of your life. Likewise, there will be longer periods of your career, perhaps even a year or two, where you will be firing on all cylinders. If you take a snapshot of your life at one of these busy moments, it may feel like things are out whack, so it is important to take the long view. Your children will not be irreparably harmed by a few evenings a week with a babysitter, or if there is a month or two where you cannot attend every sporting event.

In my experience, women tend to be more worried about work-life balance than their male counterparts. This is understandable give the unequal burden that many women bear when it comes to domestic work and child rearing. If you plan on having children and you believe you will be doing the majority of the childcare, it is important to have a plan. But this plan does not have to be leaving the workforce or taking your foot of the gas in your career. It could mean moving to be near family, paying for more childcare, or finding a job that allows you to fulfill your parenting duties. Perhaps the most important thing that a woman can do to achieve work-life balance is to find a supportive life partner who is willing to do their share.

BURNOUT

Burnout is a condition that results from chronic workplace stress and is marked by exhaustion, decreased motivation, and numbness.[8] It cannot be solved by a weekend trip or a few drinks with friends. It can cause people to quit their jobs or leave the legal profession entirely. Burnout can wreak havoc on a public interest lawyer's life and career.

Public interest lawyers are at a high risk of burnout. In addition to the stressors that everyone faces, they also have the added stress of representing distressed and traumatized clients. Many of the systems in which public interest lawyers work are inherently unfair and comically dysfunctional. If you lose, your clients may face death, financial ruin, homelessness, deportation, or incarceration.

Your clients are likely to belong to the most marginalized groups in society, people for whom a legal problem is not just a nuisance but often disrupts the very fabric of their lives. As Stephen Wexler explained decades ago:

> Poor people do not have legal problems like those of private plaintiffs and defendants in law school casebooks. People who are not poor are like casebook people. In so far as the law is concerned, they lead harmonious and settled private lives; except for their business involvement, their lives usually do not demand the skills of a lawyer. . . .Poor people do not lead settled lives into which the law seldom intrudes; they are constantly involved with the law in its most intrusive forms. . .Poverty creates an abrasive interface with society; poor people are always bumping into sharp legal things.[9]

It is extremely difficult to represent people in these circumstances without being affected in one way or another. Moreover, your clients will have had absolutely horrific things

---

[8] World Health Organization, Burn-out an "Occupational Phenomenon": International Classification of Diseases, https://www.who.int/news/item/28-05-2019-burn-out-an-occupational-phenomenon-international-classification-of-diseases (last accessed May 24, 2022).

[9] Stephen Wexler, *Practicing Law for Poor People*, 79 YALE L.J. 1049, 1049–50 (1970).

happen to them, and you maybe need to have them talk about it repeatedly. That can lead to vicarious trauma, which is a psychological response to being exposed to other people's trauma. It can be severe and debilitating and can led to burnout over time.

Deciding to be a public interest lawyer means accepting the risk that your work will at some point become harmful to your mental health. But it does not mean you have to resign yourself to doing nothing about it. You will need to develop strategies to protect yourself, which is harder than it sounds. Most public interest attorneys have high levels of empathy, which is one reason they chose their vocation. But too much empathy over time can be destructive to your mental health. Caring too much can be toxic.

In my experience, burnout tends to hit public interest lawyers at two distinct points in their careers. The first point is either in law school or shortly after starting a first job. The excitement and adrenaline rush of practicing law may sustain you for a while, but if you do not learn to manage stress and vicarious trauma, you will quickly hit a point where it becomes too much. Some common trigger events are losing a case that you think you should have won or counseling a client that their legal problem will be difficult to resolve favorably. The client will be understandably upset and may blame you even though it is not your fault. You will not get the gratitude you expect for working tirelessly on your client's behalf.

The second point is somewhere mid-career when the practice of law is no longer novel and you have seen enough to know that most societal problems have no easy answers. Perhaps you suffer a large setback on an issue you have been working on for years. You begin to feel like the effort you have put in has been futile. It is difficult to keep going.

Each of these types of burnout requires a different response. For the first kind, your goal should be to create habits that protect you from the worst of the grief that comes with representing clients. That does not mean becoming less empathetic, though that is the path that some lawyers take. Instead, you need to find some emotional distance from your empathy so that you can manage it. When I am feeling overwhelmed with stress and worry about a client, I have a few mantras I repeat to myself. My favorites are: "There are many forces outside of my control that affect what happens to my client" and "I am doing the best I can. I am only human." I know these things at this point, but sometimes I still need to remind myself of them.

Young public interest lawyers must also learn how to set healthy boundaries, which not only will help prevent burnout but also will allow you to have a better work-life balance. Clients should not be calling you at 2:00 am unless it is truly an emergency. They should not be asking you for money or to fix their non-legal problems. Some clients will push your boundaries. I once had a detained client who called 15–20 times a day no matter how often I told him that he should only call during business hours and that there were no developments in his case. When I would fail to pick up, the next time we spoke he would berate me for missing his calls. "It must be nice to be home with your family enjoying your comfortable life while I am sitting here rotting in jail," he would say. It is particularly important to maintain boundaries with these kinds of clients.

The second kind of burnout is more complex. It cannot be solved by repeating mantras or setting boundaries, because it is caused by an acknowledgment of a fundamental truth: that we are limited in what we can accomplish as individuals. Most injustices will be bigger than us and will take generations to fix. Much of the work we do as a public interest lawyer will amount to naught. Sometimes, the individual successes we have will not be enough to sustain us through dark times.

The most effective way to prevent this kind of burnout is to make sure you have good work-life balance before burnout hits. Cultivate close friendships. Read for pleasure. Travel. Start a hobby. Get married and have kids (or don't!). Do not work every second of every day, and even more importantly, have an identity that is not solely based on your profession. That way, when things seem hopeless, you will have something to fall back on. And if you feel like you are starting to burn out, do not ignore it. Take a long vacation, a sabbatical, or a leave of absence if you are able to do so financially. No one will force you to do it. If you wait until it is a crisis, it may be too late.

Law students should start developing good work habits in law school to avoid burnout later. Law school is a pressure cooker and law students often report high levels of stress and anxiety. Some of this is unavoidable, but you can manage it. Do not overcommit yourself. Take personal time. Find ways to relax. It may seem like it will get easier after law school, but it won't. Life just gets more complicated and your responsibilities to others will only increase. You must take care of yourself now so that you will be able to thrive later.

FUNDING YOUR WORK

One of the perennial problems that public interest lawyers face is how to fund their work. If you are lucky enough to get a public interest fellowship, you may be able to defer this problem for a few years, but after your fellowship ends, you will need to either get hired on at your current organization or find a new job. Both options require funding.

Depending on the organization, that may mean submitting grant applications, hosting fundraising events, or pitching individual donors. There are very few public interest lawyers who do no fundraising work. If you are one of these lawyers, consider yourself lucky.

When determining which sources of funding to apply for or accept, here are some questions you should try to answer:

(1) Does this funding support the work I want to do?

There may be times when you feel so desperate to get funded that you will agree to do almost anything. Maybe you really want to work on the problem of homelessness, but a foundation comes along that offers grants for organizations to do consumer protection work. Consumer fraud is an important issue but if you do not want to work on it, you should think twice before accepting the funding. That is not to say that you should never adjust your plan based on the funding that is available. Slight variations may pose no problem or may even add dimensions to your work. And sometimes changing directions to chase funding is unavoidable. We all need a job at the end of the day. But you should try to avoid this kind of funding if possible. You will be happier at the end of the day if you are doing work you want to be doing.

This is even more likely to happen at an organizational level. Non-profits often determine the direction of the organization not based on their mission but based on what funding they can get. This may seem like a short-term compromise to pay the bills, but it is very hard to right the ship after it has set sail.

When I was working at a public interest organization, we thought about funding using this chart:

The left axis indicates whether the work you are considering taking on is within the organization's mission or not. The top axis indicates whether the work is funded. Ideally, an organization would only do work that is both within its mission and funded (1). If that is impossible, it will need to take on some work that is central to its mission but does not come with its own funding (2). To fund this work, the organization may need to do some work that is not within its core mission, but that is funded (3). And an organization should avoid at all costs work that is neither central to the mission nor funded (4). You can think about funding your own job in the same way.

(2) Does this funding come with restrictions that will present obstacles to doing the work?

Sometimes, you find a funding opportunity that sounds great until you look at the fine print. The quintessential example of this is LSC funding, which can fund a broad range of legal services but which comes with restrictions you may not be happy with. Foundations, too, may have restrictions on what work they will fund, as do government grants. Some state and local funding cannot be used to represent people with criminal records, for instance. If you do not want to abide by those restrictions, then you should not accept the funding. Again, if this is your only option, you might have to suck it up and deal with the restrictions, but you should do an honest assessment of how much of an obstacle they will pose for your work if you accept it.

Even when there are not explicit restrictions on funding, organizations may feel constrained in the positions they take or the work they take on because they fear upsetting funders. A common example is criticizing a state or local government while relying on government grants or taking on an unpopular client that is likely to garner you unflattering press. This self censorship can be just as problematic as grant restrictions and should be taken into account before accepting funding. Ask yourself: "Will I feel free to make independent decisions about the work I take on?" If not, it should give you pause.

(3) Is the funding tied to reasonable outcomes?

Before accepting any funding, make sure that the funder has realistic expectations for what can be achieved with the amount provided. You would not agree to a grant that gives you $5,000 to build a rocket ship to the moon and you should not accept a grant that asks you to represent 60 people in complex litigation for the same amount. One easy way to think about this is to figure out what percentage of an individual lawyer's time in a year would be required to achieve the outcome. Taking the previous example, let's say you calculate that it will take at least 25% of a lawyer's time in a year to represent sixty people (the actual percentage is probably much higher). If the grant amount is $5,000, that works out to a salary of $20,000 per year. Are you making more than that? If so, then the grant is not adequately paying for your time. I have seen countless organizations make this mistake. They cobble together a bunch of grants that each have unreasonable expectations. The organization can only meet the grant requirements by overworking its staff, which can lead to burnout and attrition.

At the largest organizations, you may have fundraising staff who are making these decisions for you. If so, you need to communicate with them to ensure that the funding they accept works for you. They may also have ideas for how to juggle things so that you can accept the funding while finding ways to do the work you want to do. Non-profits live and breathe on this kind of creative accounting.

As a public interest lawyer, securing funding will be a part of your job. But it is the work that should drive the fundraising, not the other way around.

CHAPTER 7

MID-CAREER

This section is not really for practicing public interest lawyers. After all, by the time you have been a lawyer for a few years, you have become the expert in your own career. You are probably sharing your wisdom with younger lawyers. You do not need general career advice from a book. There is one group of lawyers, though, who may benefit from some guidance in the middle of their career: lawyers who did not become public interest lawyers but who now want to incorporate public interest law into their practice. They could be wanting to do more pro bono legal work in their current job or they could be looking to change career paths entirely. It is never too late to become a public interest lawyer. This chapter will teach you how.

PUBLIC INTEREST WORK IN PRIVATE PRACTICE

All lawyers should engage in public interest lawyering of some kind. Even lawyers who decide they cannot or do not want to pursue a public interest legal career must find ways to do pro bono legal work that contributes to the public good. It is a moral obligation we have as members of the legal profession. It should be non-negotiable.

Although all lawyers are encouraged to engage in pro bono work—the Model Rules of Professional Conduct state that lawyers should aspire to provide 50 hours of pro bono legal services per year[1]—there is no jurisdiction that currently requires lawyers to do any pro bono at all. Consequently, many lawyers do not. A 2017 survey by the American Bar Association found that 48% of respondents had not done any pro bono work in the past year and 20% had never undertaken pro bono service of any kind.[2] The average number of hours spent providing pro

[1] American Bar Association, Model Rules of Professional Conduct, Rule 6.1 ("Every lawyer has a professional responsibility to provide legal services to those unable to pay. A lawyer should aspire to render at least (50) hours of pro bono publico legal services per year.").

[2] American Bar Association, Supporting Justice: A Report on the Pro Bono Work of America's Lawyers 5 (2018), *available at* https://www.americanbar.org/content/dam/

bono services for all lawyers was 36.9 per year,[3] a number that obscures the fact that a small number of lawyers do an extraordinary amount of pro bono work while others do almost none.

Some of the lawyers who fail to do pro bono are solo practitioners or lawyers working in small firms who feel they cannot devote themselves to non-paying work for fear of falling into the red. Others may have personal reasons why they cannot take on pro bono work in a given year—a medical diagnosis, a mental health condition, or other extenuating personal situations.

However, these excuses do not explain why more than 50% of lawyers do no pro bono work whatsoever in a given year. Something more fundamental is going on. Obviously, many lawyers do not believe that they have an obligation to use their legal skills to contribute to the public good, except in the narrow sense that they represent their clients diligently, work to hone their craft, and contribute to the well-functioning of the legal system.

This is simply unacceptable. Lawyers have a special obligation to the public interest, either by devoting ourselves to public interest careers or, at the very least, by spending a significant amount of time providing pro bono legal services. It is not sufficient for lawyers to contribute to their communities in other ways, for example by volunteering or donating money to charity. There is nothing wrong with this kind of contribution and we should applaud people who devote themselves to the greater good no matter what form it takes. But only lawyers can provide pro bono legal services, which means they have a moral obligation to do so.

Lawyers play a unique role in the legal system and have a skill set that no one else has. The legal system controls almost every aspect of our lives, particularly for low-income and marginalized communities. Lawyers created this system and we serve as its gatekeepers. Given that, our obligation extends

---

aba/administrative/probono_public_service/ls_pb_supporting_justice_iv_final.authcheckdam.pdf.

[3] *Id.*

beyond that of an ordinary person to ensure that the system is fair and just.

That does not mean that every lawyer must strive to be Thurgood Marshall. There is other legal work to do and not enough public interest jobs for everyone. But that does not absolve lawyers of the responsibility that comes with being a lawyer. We have a tremendous amount of privilege granted to us by the legal system. In return, we must challenge the system when it fails people, which it often does.

The legal profession must get more serious about pushing all lawyers to provide pro bono legal services. State bar committees should consider putting in place mandatory pro bono requirements, subject to waivers for extenuating circumstances. State and local bar associations already coordinate pro bono programs. More resources must be poured into these programs. Law schools, too, must impress upon law students that this is their professional responsibility.

If you work in the private sector, there are many ways to incorporate pro bono or public interest work into your practice. The simplest way is to take on a pro bono client in an area of law that you are interested in. Many larger firms have pro bono coordinators who identify and pre-vet pro bono opportunities for their lawyers. If you work at a firm or company that does not provide this service, you can reach out to local public interest organizations and ask them for referrals. Most organizations have more work than they can realistically take on. As mentioned, bar associations are another good source of pro bono opportunities.

You might decide to dabble in a bunch of different kinds of pro bono work, or you may decide to specialize, becoming the person that public interest organizations come to when they need co-counsel on impact litigation. Some of the most monumental civil rights cases of the last few decades were brought by law firm lawyers, usually in conjunction with public interest organizations. For example, *U.S. v. Windsor*, the Supreme Court case that struck down the Defense of Marriage Act (DOMA) was litigated and argued by Roberta Kaplan, then a partner at Paul, Weiss, Rifkind, Wharton & Garrison LLP.[4] Seth Waxman, a partner at Wilmer Cutler Pickering Hale and Dorr LLP, argued and won *Boumediene v. Bush*, which established that individuals held at Guantanamo Bay had the right to file habeas corpus petitions.[5] These are prominent examples, but there are many other lawyers in the private sector who have taken on important impact cases and won.

You may also decide to develop a close relationship with a single public interest organization whose work you can support on an ongoing basis. This may mean providing different kinds of resources: pro bono legal services, in-kind donations, consulting, fundraising. You may end up with an invitation to join the organization's board, which can give you a platform to affect the future direction of the organization's work.

If you are working at a law firm, you may wonder how you will have time to fit pro bono work into your already hectic schedule. Your paying clients will not accept less than one hundred percent of your attention. Your firm may require you to spend so many hours on paid work that there is hardly time left to sleep, let alone take on a pro bono case. These are real challenges, but they are surmountable.

The most important thing you can do is choose to work at a law firm that values pro bono work. This does not just mean that the firm says it values it. Talk is cheap. Instead, you should look at the firm's policies to see whether they realistically allow people to devote some of their time to pro bono opportunities. The higher the annual billable hour requirements, the less feasible it is to take on substantial pro bono clients. The same goes for law firms who do not count pro bono hours towards the billable hour requirement. There are firms out there that value pro bono work. You just have to make sure that you go work for one of them.

Firms should implement policies that do not just allow associates to count a certain number of hours to pro bono work, but that require it. The policy would mandate that at least some

---

[4] ROBERTA KAPLAN, THEN COMES MARRIAGE (2015).

[5] Seth P. Waxman, https://www.wilmerhale.com/en/people/seth-waxman (last accessed May 24, 2022).

percentage (10–15%) of billable hours must be spent on pro bono matters. Making it a requirement will give associates the freedom to take advantage of the policies without worrying about failing to fulfill their other obligations or disappointing supervisors. Until firms adopt these kinds of policies, however, it will be up to individual lawyers to make it happen.

Once you join a law firm, you will need to make it a personal priority to find pro bono opportunities. If you do not make it a priority, it will not happen. If you wait until things calm down and you have extra time, you will never do it. The strange thing about time is that it tends to expand when you need it to. You will find time to work on your pro bono matters.

If you are a solo practitioner or a lawyer working at a small law firm with thin margins, you can still do public interest work. Although "pro bono" has become synonymous with "free legal services," the original Latin phrase, "pro bono publico," simply means "for the public good." You can take on paid work that is for the public good. One way to do this is to do "low bono" work, which means legal services in which you charge below market rates. Many private public interest law firms use this model, but any lawyer can do it. You can also take on legal challenges with the possibility of attorney's fees. If you win, the opposing party can pay your bills.

Any lawyer can do pro bono work if they make it a priority. Every lawyer should consider themselves a public interest lawyer—at least some of the time.

TRANSITIONING TO PUBLIC INTEREST LATER

Many law students make the decision to go to a law firm for a few years, pay off their student loans, and then transition to another job they like more. It is possible to do this, but it is not as easy as they think it will be.

From the students' perspective, this decision makes a lot of sense. What's the harm in going to work at a law firm for a couple of years when you can pay off your debt, get some good legal experience, and still spend most of your career in public interest? What is a few years in the grand scheme of things?

From the perspective of potential public interest employers, however, the decision is problematic. You have signaled that public interest work is not that important to you. If it were, you would have gone into public interest law right out of law school. The majority of public interest lawyers also have or had student loans and they figured out a way to pay them without a law firm salary. They are not going to be sympathetic to the argument that you needed to pay off your loans. Public interest lawyers are a very judgmental bunch; do not expect them to agree with your decision to go make a lot of money.

As for that legal experience? Many public interest lawyers have a fairly low opinion of the training that law firm associates get in their first couple years. There is a belief, rightly or wrongly, that most new associates spend a lot of time doing grunt work before being given real responsibility. Public interest organizations cannot wait years before giving their attorneys such responsibility, and they have a high opinion of the training they provide.

Moreover, the skills you learn at a firm may not translate well. Skills like how to do e-discovery are little used in public interest practice. Nor are you likely to have the chance to learn things like trauma-informed lawyering and how to work with people living in poverty. In addition, firm lawyers learn to practice law with almost limitless financial resources at their disposal. Public interest lawyering requires a different skill set.

It should be said that this prejudice against corporate lawyers exists much more in some spheres than in others. Government agencies usually do not care whether you spent time in the private sector and may even see it as an advantage. Private public interest law firms are also likely to forgive a previous stint at a big corporate firm, though you will still need to convince them that you believe in the mission of the firm. Prosecutors often spend time in the private sector. Public defenders occasionally do too, as evidenced by recently-confirmed Supreme Court Justice Kentanji Brown-Jackson's resume.[6] Corporate lawyers will face the most scrutiny if they

---

[6] Amy Howe, *Profile of a Potential Nominee: Ketanji Brown Jackson*, SCOTUS BLOG, Feb. 1 2022, available at https://www.scotusblog.com/2022/02/profile-of-a-potential-nominee-ketanji-brown-jackson.

want to go work for a non-profit organization for the reasons I outlined above.

If you want to transition from a law firm to a public interest organization, all hope is not lost. What can you do to maximize your chances of a successful transition? First and foremost, you should be planning your exit on the very first day of orientation at your law firm. Do not lose focus on your ultimate goal if you want a shot at reaching it.

The first thing you should do is devote as much time as you can to doing pro bono work in the area that you eventually want to transition to. You will be getting pressure to do more paid work than you feel like you can comfortably do—it is part of the business model. In this environment, it can feel like you simply don't have time to add pro bono work on top of your other case load.

Despite these challenges, to have any chance of successfully transitioning to public interest law, you have to devote yourself to pro bono work. If you do not, it signals to potential public interest employers that you simply do not care enough. And because you went to work at a firm, they are already operating under that assumption. You come in at a disadvantage and you need to prove them wrong.

Some law firm associates would like to do pro bono but worry that although the firm policies permit them to do so that it is frowned upon and will negatively affect future opportunities at the law firm. I wish I could say that this does not happen, but it is true that at some law firms, doing a lot of pro bono makes it harder to become a partner. This is a real problem for lawyers who would like to make partner but also want to do pro bono. But if you know that you are not on the partner track and that you are just working at a law firm to pay off your loans, it does not matter what anyone in the firm thinks about your pro bono commitment. They will not fire you right now and by the time it would become an issue, you will be long gone. Nor should you feel bad doing the minimum required on your paid work to meet the firm's annual billable hours requirements. The firm is still getting its money's worth.

After you have an active pro bono docket, you need to strategize ways to make connections with organizations that are working on issues you care about. Volunteer. Donate money. Go to annual fundraising galas and networking events. People are less likely to stereotype you as a corporate lawyer if they know you. They might even tell a hiring committee, "He is at a firm, but I've met him and he's passionate about our work." A single good word can do more than almost anything else.

Third, and perhaps most importantly, live frugally even though you are making lots of money. Pay off your loans quickly and transition to another job as soon as possible. (Living frugally will also make the transition to a public interest salary easier. Beware of the golden handcuffs.) Avoid waiting to make the move when you are 5–7 years into your firm job. Public interest organizations know about the timeline for making partner. If you leave when other people are getting pushed out, organizations will assume you are just looking for a job and that you do not really care about their work.

What if you did not leave law school with a plan to transition into public interest later, but you realize at some point mid-career that that is what you want to do? Hopefully, you have taken my advice and are already doing pro bono work. If so, once you realize what your goal is, you can double down and focus even more on the pro bono relationships you have already developed. If not, you will need to follow the advice above. It may be harder to develop a robust pro bono practice if you are mid-career lawyer who has never shown much interest in it, but it is still possible.

Another option might be to transition into another kind of public interest job, such as in government or for a private public interest law firm, and then use that as a steppingstone to get a job in a public interest organization. The further in the past your time at a law firm is, the less it will matter to public interest organizations.

What you should not do is quit your job and then assume you will waltz into a public interest job. It will not happen. You will either end up taking a job in-house at a corporation or going to another law firm. You must be humble about your experience as a law firm lawyer. You may think you are gracing the public interest world with your presence, but in truth, you have a high hill to climb.

In sum, you can transition to public interest work later in your career, but don't assume it will be easy. It takes planning and hard work to pull it off.

CHAPTER 8

CONCLUSION

Why do people become lawyers? Some do it for the money. Others see the work as intellectually challenging. But many aspiring lawyers, including most of the people reading this book, think that it provides a pathway to doing meaningful work that makes the world a better place.

Unfortunately, meaningful world-changing work is harder to come by than you might think. We often think of the pursuit of justice as being a central pillar of our legal system. Most legal work, however, does not get us any closer to a just society. In the best-case scenario, the legal system merely facilitates wealth-building by corporations and rich people and moves piles of money from one place to another, lubricating the gears of capitalism.[1]

Sometimes, its goals are explicitly counter to the pursuit of justice. Law firms make their money defending against all kinds of unsavory conduct by corporations. They have defended asbestos and tobacco companies to insulate them from paying for the harm they have caused people.[2] They represent fossil fuel companies in their quest to avoid accountability for their CO2 emissions. They represent banks in class actions alleging consumer fraud. Transactional lawyers are not off the hook either. Structuring corporate deals to avoid taxes may seem morally neutral until you think about the downstream consequences of corporations failing to pay taxes.

Many lawyers happily do this work. They do not aspire for more. They just want an interesting job that allows them to gain mastery in their profession and earn a good salary. Many legal jobs can give you that. These lawyers justify the work they do in one way or another or they simply do not think about the moral

---

1 KATHERINE PISOR, THE CODE OF CAPITAL 159 (2019).

2 Mark Hansen, *Shook Hardy Smoke 'Em*, ABA JOURNAL, Oct. 1, 2008, *available at* https://www.abajournal.com/magazine/article/shook_hardy_smokes_em.

valence of their work at all. Are you one of these people? Is that the work you want to do? If so, carry on.

If not, it is time to make some hard choices. Your career will be long, but not infinitely so. Every decision you make opens up some opportunities while foreclosing others. We like to avoid thinking about our lives in this way because if we dwell on it too much, it can lead to paralysis. But to ignore it altogether creates another problem. We make consequential life decisions without realizing we are doing so. Law school is a crossroads in your life. It is here that your professional identity as a lawyer is forged. You will leave law school a different person than you entered it and set out on a path of your own design. What will that path be?

I want to make a modest proposition: you should believe in what you do. True, you could go make a lot of money with a plan to find your way back to what you really want to do at some point in the future. But why waste a few years of your life in a job you dislike? Why not just decide that you are going to do work you believe in from the beginning?

I hope this book has taught you that it is possible to have a rewarding, successful public interest career and still live a good life. In fact, finding purpose in your work is what makes a good life possible. If you make the decision to become a public interest lawyer, I hope this book helps you accomplish your goals. The public interest career of your dreams is within your reach.